In_

Break Free From What Holds You Back

By: Anna Light

Published by:

2410 W. Memorial Rd.
Suite C #260
Oklahoma City, OK 73134
nxtlevel.net

ISBN: 9780988209640
Printed in the United States of America Library
of Congress Cataloging in-Publication Data

Table of Contents

Scripture references are from the New International Version (NIV), unless otherwise indicated.

Some names have been changed to protect the privacy of the individuals.

Foreword

Pastor Amy Groeschel

Co-founder of Life.Church

Co-author of *From This Day Forward* and *SOAR*

Security – a confidence that comes from feeling safe and free from fear – is not a luxury, it is a vital and basic human need.

Security heals us emotionally as well as physically. Security is like a sheep experiencing the care of a good shepherd – like that of our Psalm 23 God. Security is the confidence to live knowing that God's goodness and mercy will follow you.

But too often, and for all sorts of reasons, fear and anxiety are commonplace in the human heart, and the root of these two ominous emotions is insecurity.

Do you know, without a doubt, that you are infinitely loved? Do you know that you have value that is far beyond what you produce, look like, or even act like?

I would long have answered, "Yes, of course, I know I am loved." But now I know these Truths in a far deeper and more personal way. God uniquely revealed them to me through various difficult circumstances. Now I shout a resounding, *"Yes! God loves me! I am His and He is mine. Nothing could ever separate me from His love."* Above all else, knowing and experiencing God's love sets us free. The more we gain a better grasp of His indescribable love, the greater freedom we live in.

Anna Light isn't too different from you and me. She's known the thrill of romance and success, but she's also tasted the bitterness of disappointment and rejection. What makes Anna a standout in the crowd is her newly found freedom in Christ. And not just the amazing freedom that came from her faith in Christ, but a growing freedom of discovering her true value because of Christ.

In_Security was born in Anna's heart because of her obedient compassion to serve others by teaching them the same truths that transformed her heart and mind.

The book you're holding is full of potential. With God's help, it has the potential to open your eyes to view yourself as God sees you. It has the potential to break the strongholds of lies that you've believed about yourself. It can potentially bring you a level of freedom that you've never known before. My prayer is that *In_Security* will be your new normal.

May you know that you are wonderfully fashioned by our glorious God. May you overflow with courage, love, faith, hope, compassion, and dignity - just to name a few - because Christ Jesus came to bring us the good news that through His amazing grace we are chosen, loved, and adored... His very Own!

Introduction

The old idiom "Better late than never" is appropriate here. This book has been writing itself in my brain over the last ten years. I've worked on it, agonized over it, hated it, loved it, needed it. There were times I gave up on finishing it for the very reason I felt called to write it. Ironic, isn't it? Insecure about writing a book about insecurity. The inadequacy I've felt while writing has only fueled the fire I have to help others overcome the insecurities holding them back. I see others struggling under the weight of insecurity, living in lies, and being held back from their full capacity, and I realize that yes, I must finish it no matter how long it might take. I have to remind myself that I really don't care what people think—or at least I'm not supposed to care. But I do. We all do. We care and compare and judge and believe things that aren't true, and therein lies my desire to get this story out. God has called me to help people overcome the insecurities that hold them back, so I choose again to honor his calling and get to work.

Sometimes I look up quotations about writing to inspire myself before I start, and the one I read today expresses how I feel about this subject. "A real writer doesn't just want to write; a real writer has to write." The urge gnaws at me until I have no excuses left. This story has to be told, even if it's just to remind me what I know. But I believe God's timing is perfect, that someone reading this book needs to hear these words. You've lived in the shadow of your own insecurity for too long and it is your time to walk into the light, liberated from your bondage. For you, I write. If you have ever felt stuck in your abilities, drained by life's circumstances, wrought up from self-hate, or held back from a full and vibrant life by an indefinable weight of fear, this book is for you.

But why must a book like this be written? Why is there so much bondage in people's lives— to sin, depression, fear, anxiety, self-destructive behaviors, insecurity and lies? I believe it is because the enemy knows the most powerful person on the planet—and the most dangerous to him—is a free person, a person set free by the death and resurrection of Jesus Christ, a person who is able to rise above the lies that bind her and walk in the Truth of who she is. Our enemy is threatened by our power and influence, so he's doing everything he can to keep us bound up, focused on the wrong things, and wallowing in despair. When we're free, we're not held back by fear, self-doubt or self-hate. When we're free there are endless possibilities for God to work in and through us to accomplish all He's called us to do. The enemy doesn't want us free. That is the very reason we must become free.

Here's how this book can help get you to that freedom. In the first section, "Problem, Prison, Pain", we will define insecurity in its various forms, finally putting a name to what it is we are fighting. Once we have laid the foundation, we will build on our knowledge in section two, "Presence, Perception, Power", and learn how to stop living our lives for the approval of others. By section three, "Promise, Pursuit, Prize", you will have the tools you need to break free from the insecurities holding you back, launching your capacity and influence to the next level.

As I share my journey I give you the framework to begin your own journey to freedom. At the end of each chapter we will Take a Deeper Step In_Security. This is an opportunity for you to write out your own thoughts and personalize the framework to fit your unique struggle. There will be times I ask you to stop reading and do an exercise. There will be time and space for you to engage in the material, apply it to your life, and see the lasting effects as you put it into practice. But before we get there I want to make one thing clear. Trying to find freedom from insecurity without a relationship with Jesus Christ is like jumping out of an airplane without a parachute. He is the creator of your heart, the founder of your life. If you're looking to rid yourself of the chains that keep you bound, your relationship with Him needs to be the center of your life. Whether you've known His grace before, or never known it at all, it is ready and waiting for you to accept as your own and begin the journey to become the person He designed you to be.

It's time to become free. Let's become dangerous to the enemy.

Part 1

Problem

Prison

Pain

One

You Didn't Choose Me, You Got Stuck with Me

"You're fat!" Those two words came from a boy named Stephen when I was in the fifth grade. When he said them, a strange feeling came over me. I remember it to this day; I got hot all over and felt my cheeks flush. My heart pounded fast in my ears and I felt panicked. Not knowing what else to do, I threw an equally hurtful put-down in his face before turning away to hide my tears.

I tried to act like his words didn't affect me, but they did. I choked back the tears, mortified to realize that other people were thinking the same thing I thought about myself. I knew I was fat. But to hear it from another person cut me deeper than I cared to recognize. If someone else thought I was fat, it must be who I was.

I don't remember the exact time I started putting on weight, but I do know that food was always a big deal to me. I'd like to blame it on the fact that I grew up as the fourth of seven children, right smack dab in the middle. I'd like to say my fascination and need for food came from a feeling that if I did not make sure I got enough to eat then I wouldn't eat. As the middle child it seemed like it would be easy for others to forget about me. But if I said living in a big family was the reason I grew up overweight, I wouldn't be telling the truth. The truth was that I developed an addiction to food and the comfort it brought me when I ate.

My obsession for eating, mixed with the inability to control myself caused my weight to spiral out of control. My lack of self-control was a source of shame in my life that I couldn't hide. When you're overweight, your problem is on display for all to see. At least that's how I felt. By the time I was eighteen I weighed well over two hundred pounds, which was considered clinically obese for my height and body composition. Those two little words from Stephen back in the fifth grade continued to haunt me. As I grew up I always wondered who else thought them, who else said them under their breath, or to a friend once my back was turned. Those words were the filter of my interactions with people. I was never really able to be myself. I was never fully "present" because in the back of my mind the question kept buzzing around like a little fly: "Do they think

I'm fat?" This deep shame drove me away from healthy relationships. I kept people at arm's length because I was embarrassed by my lack of control. I isolated myself, and developed social anxiety that left me crippled. The only comfort I felt was when I was eating. It dulled the pain and made me forget, if only for a moment, how much I hated who I was becoming.

Growing up, I always felt like I was in this strange tug-of-war. My heart was full of wonderful dreams, and I felt the call of God on my life to do great things for Him, but my mind kept telling me I would never amount to anything. I didn't feel special, but average. I grew up in a Christian home with good parents. I was home schooled, met Jesus when I was six-years-old and never strayed from His path. I didn't have an earth-shattering testimony and because I never did anything, I felt I would never do anything for God. How could God use me? I really had nothing to offer. Add to that, my weight held me back from my full potential. I didn't like myself, so I assumed no one else did either.

I allowed those thoughts to hold me back from many things as I grew older. As a high school student there were countless opportunities to be athletic and play games with friends. But more often than not, I found myself sitting out, playing the role of the "cheerleader" instead of being a part of the action. Even though I wanted so badly to play, I was more afraid of what people would think if I did.

I remember one Fourth of July a group of friends got together to hang out. They wanted to play ultimate Frisbee and there was a perfect field for it where we were. The group pressured me into playing. The team captains started choosing their players and I can remember what was going through my head as I waited. *Why did I decide to play? No one is going to pick me. I'm horrible at this game. I'm no good at sports. No one will want me on their team. I'll probably make us lose. I should just sit out and save everyone the trouble.* As I was thinking these thoughts I heard my name. I snapped out of my silent monologue and looked around me. Sure enough, I was the last one standing. The last one chosen.

"Come on," one of my friends said, "We choose you."

As I walked to the circle I felt like Rachel Green on the episode of *Friends* when they were playing football during Thanksgiving and chose her last... *"You didn't choose me, you got stuck with me! I'm a reject."*

That was the last time I decided to play anything. I couldn't run without quickly getting out of breath and I was always too afraid to take any kind of risks. *What would people think? I don't belong in this group. They probably wish I wasn't even here.* Those thoughts controlled most of my thinking growing up.

The shame kept me down and kept me quiet, because it wasn't only in sports that I held myself back. Often times, in group settings I would know the answer to a question, but I wouldn't say anything for fear that maybe I was wrong, or that people would think I was trying to be a know-it-all. Maybe if I just kept my mouth shut I could somewhat control how others thought of me, but even that was not possible. I continued feeling passed over as the spear of rejection dug deeper into my heart. My sister and I were close growing up and always shared the same friends. When one of those friends had a birthday party and could only invite a certain number of people she chose my sister instead of me. A seemingly insignificant and childish memory, but one that only seemed to confirm what I believed about myself - no one likes me and no one wants to be around me.

I'll never forget being at a wedding and watching all the beautiful girls out on the dance floor. I taught myself not to hope because rejection was too painful. I stood against the wall desperately longing to be out there but also wishing I was invisible. I couldn't get past the fear that seemed to paralyze my every move. I hated myself. I hated that I allowed the fear of rejection to hold me back. I hated that I seemed to live my life for everyone but me, always fearing what people would think. I hated that the only thing that made me feel better was food, the very thing that first put me in this situation.

I remember one afternoon I was in my bedroom doing a workout, trying to be healthy and turn things around, when all of a sudden a new thought woke in my mind with each lift of the five-pound weight. *I'm always going to be like this. I'll never lose weight. No wonder no one wants to be around me. I'm so ugly. Give up! There's no use in trying. I'll never amount to anything. I should just end it all right now. It would be so much easier.*

I wanted to throw the weights through the window, but instead I dropped them to the floor, lay on my bed and sobbed. I wanted to die. I didn't want to live anymore. I started thinking of ways I might end my life. Contemplating suicide seemed logical. How else could I escape the taunting that seemed to originate from inside me? I felt like I was drowning. I couldn't get air. Something must be wrong with me.

Those dark days lasted far too long. In my junior and senior years of high school I started having heart problems. Without warning, my heart would start to pound too fast. I had to stop what I was doing and wait for it to slow down and take deep breaths or sometimes cough a certain way for it to get back to normal. It was like a panic attack that left me physically exhausted. Sometimes the attack would last five seconds, sometimes five minutes. After it was over I felt as if I had just run a race as fast as I could. I didn't know what to think. After a few episodes we went to the doctor so he could monitor my heart.

He told us it was a condition called supra-ventricular tachy-cardia — stress induced. I was causing physical problems in my body by my inability to control my thoughts and emotions. I didn't know what was causing it or what to do but I did know that something had to change. I knew there was more inside me than I was showing. I knew I was capable of being more, but something was always holding me back. I felt trapped. I began to realize this was not just a weight issue, it was something far deeper.

Ultimately I began to seek God for answers. He revealed to me that my weight and the shame that accompanied it were only symptoms of a much deeper issue brewing beneath the surface. As I prayed and searched and pleaded, God revealed to me that I couldn't keep treating the symptoms. I had to deal with the root problem. When I finally submitted myself to His leadership, instead of trying to fix myself on my own, He revealed to me what it was I was fighting. Insecurity.

Okay, so, I'm struggling with insecurity. But what does that mean exactly? Over the years I studied this word *insecurity*. Webster's dictionary explains insecurity as: *not confident or sure, uncertain, not adequately guarded or sustained, not firmly fastened or fixed.* The definition revealed a great deal about my behavior. What do people do when they lack confidence? They are untrusting. What if they are not sure, uncertain, or doubtful? They are cautious and held back. What if they don't feel protected? They attack. That is definitely the way I felt most of the time; wandering through life, blown around by the opinion of others and never sure where I was going or what I was doing, prostituting my emotions to anyone who would give me a little attention, seeking validation in any way I could. As I began to pay more attention to this word, I began to catch myself in its behavior. It was more than being overweight; it was more than random panic attacks or social anxiety. Those were only signs of a bigger issue. It was a deeper problem reaching down into the core of who I was, and it was not just my problem either. It was, and is, a human problem manifesting itself in as many different ways as the individuals it infects. How is it sinking its teeth into you?

Take a deeper step: In_Security

1. Rewrite the definition of insecurity in your own words.

   Lack of self confidence
   Focus on inward lacks

2. Take a moment and think about your own behavior over the past couple months. What do you do when you lack confidence?

   I think negatively and sometimes talk negatively. Can project confidence even though I'm hurting

3. How does it make you feel when you are uncertain or doubtful about yourself or a decision you need to make?

   Whats wrong? Why can't I make a simple decision

4. How do you act when you feel threatened or insecure?

   I pretend I'm ok

5. Rate yourself on a scale of 1-10 (one being least) how secure do you feel as you begin this journey? Explain your answer:

   1   2   3   4   5   ⑥   7   8   9   10

23

Two

I'm not alone

Over the last few years, as I have observed those around me, I have discovered we are a people caught up in the sticky web of insecurity. Everyone struggles with some form of insecurity or another. It is not gender specific, age specific, career or weight specific. It is a menacing evil that builds like a tropical storm, making the air around us thick with doubt, worry, fear, and poor self-esteem. It dates back all the way to the beginning of the human race when Adam and Eve decided to take matters into their own hands and sin against God. They were deceived by the Father of Lies himself. When we believe a lie it is like taking a bite of that forbidden fruit, just as they did. After they were deceived, they felt naked, exposed, afraid, insecure. They wanted to cover themselves for security, to hide behind a mask that made them feel safer, but it was never enough. And it's still not enough today. No matter what we do to hide our fears, no matter how we try to mask our insecurities, they always have a way of showing themselves through the poorly constructed coverings we create in our lives. How can we overcome insecurity? How do we live free from it?

The years from eighteen to twenty-one are what I call my transformation years. True, most young adults change dramatically during that period, but for me it was a life-changing transformation, not only mentally as I grew more mature, but spiritually, emotionally and physically as I dove into a calling I felt the Lord had given me. At eighteen, after I began to understand the struggle of insecurity, I was given the opportunity to speak to a hundred Junior High girls in a three-week series about insecurity. This is when I began to realize that I wasn't the only one struggling to live free. Many of the students and leaders involved in that series wrote to me about the fears, worries and doubts they struggled with daily. That was the first time I felt prompted to start keeping notes about my observations of insecurity.

A year later I met a girl named Britney. I didn't fully understand this girl. You see she had a weight problem, but instead of allowing her weight to make her fade into the background, like it did me, this girl craved the limelight, the exact opposite behavior I was used to experiencing. Not only did she love the limelight, she might have been one of the loudest and most

26

obnoxious persons I had ever met. How strange. This girl's insecurity manifested itself differently from mine, but the root problem was the same. I felt like I was on to something.

As I continued to invest in figuring out how to overcome this problem, God brought many different people into my life. I felt like he almost gave me two sets of eyes, one to see the physical, visible person just like everyone else sees, and one to see the heart, the deeper side of why people are the way they are and why they act the way they do.

Silvia Burman is a perfect example. I first met Silvia at a Christian writer's conference in 2005. I was still struggling with my weight, but Silvia was one of the fittest, most beautiful people I'd ever met. We hit it off right away, spending extra time together at the conference even after our meetings were over. I admired her for her beauty and physique but I began to realize Silvia had a problem, too. Almost every word that came out of her mouth was negative. There was a critical spirit that seemed to hover over her like a storm cloud. She was thirty-three years old and had never been married. According to her, she probably would never be married. Every guy was a jerk and no man, as far as she was concerned, was going to live up to her standards or expectations. She was one of those people who had made up her mind ten years ago and nothing anyone else could say would change it. Being a natural encourager I tried several times to help her see a different way of thinking but she had an answer or excuse for everything. She was so critical and judgmental I was beginning to realize why she held herself to such a standard of perfection. Being better than everyone else made her feel secure. It was her poorly constructed covering and I began to see straight through it. It got to be quite exhausting, so I finally realized I just needed to shut my mouth and listen. "I'm just stuck," she said. "I feel like giving up. This is not the life I expected to be living at thirty-three."

I listened, nodding every few minutes. I sensed a real struggle in her. There was an unhappiness about her spirit, a negativity that was palpable. Instead of allowing her to bring me down, I began to see her heart and how much she hurt. I thought beautiful, skinny girls didn't have any problems; they didn't have to worry about how they looked or how many carbs they could eat in a day. But I realized something from that interaction— insecurity comes in many different forms. There was something in this girl's life that was holding her back from the life she expected to be living. Seeing her behavior for what it really was enabled me to care about her when others might just write her off as hateful. Yes, our outside issues were different, but there was a common thread that laced through the deeper problem.

The Journey Continued

After serving as a leader for my church's youth ministry for two years, a youth pastor internship opened up and one of my mentors encouraged me to apply. I was unsure at first. I was supposed to become a writer, but I knew I loved ministry as well, so I took a leap of faith with confidence I didn't feel and I was accepted. The internship itself was transforming and difficult. I not only learned to face my fear of public speaking, but realized I loved getting in front of people and preaching God's Word. I had many people encourage my development along the way and I gained valuable knowledge about leadership, but it was what God was doing in me personally during this time that truly left me a different person. I felt God's prompting to get myself ready for what He had for me in the next season. I had to figure out a way to put the fear and self-doubt behind me, to shed whatever it was that held me back from answering the call God placed on my life. I found myself, quite often, pouring hours into His Word looking for answers because it was the only place I knew to look. I gained much confidence through what I read, and continued making notes about how I was overcoming my insecurities, filing them away for later use, knowing at some point I would share them with others. I was changing.

Nine months into the internship a position became available at a new Life.Church campus. I went through the interview process which was rigid and designed to reveal the true person behind each candidate, pulling them out of their comfort zones. I had to jump off the precipice called "playing it safe"—I had lived there too long—and jump into the chasm of the unknown. This was a huge step for me. Even in 2007, Life.Church was one of the largest churches in America. I felt inadequate to be considered for a position, but another feeling, bigger than my inadequacy, pulled at me to make the jump. It had to be God's calling and plan because at the end of the interview the campus pastor, Scott Williams, took a risk on me—a twenty-year-old female—and I was hired at Life.Church as a youth pastor. He saw my potential, maybe before I saw it myself. He believed in me. Something awakened inside of me when I realized someone else believed in me. I felt a confidence begin to bloom. Under his leadership and the transformative culture of the staff at Life.Church, I continued to become a different person. So at the ripe old age of twenty, I had countless opportunities to minister to men and women about this overwhelming sickness of insecurity and share my thoughts and ideas even as I was experiencing them first hand.

I first met Travis at a youth ministry leader night. He wanted to get involved in serving with students. At first glance he seemed to be an amazing leader. Always showed up, always on time, always consistent. He loved the kids and he was great with them, but I always felt he was covering something up, or hiding from something. I felt he could never show the real him, that he always had to make sure I knew how well he was doing. He craved approval at every turn and made sure he got it one way or another. It was as if the praise of other people was the fuel that kept him going. I began to realize this was another manifestation of insecurity.

I'll never forget Sherri. The girl was a mess and she knew it. After being molested at the age of twelve she was never the same. Hard, ruthless, calloused and dying from the inside out, Sherri changed relationships like she changed shoes. Every few months it was someone different. She slept with every one of them, addicted to sex, or the feeling of love it brought even for a brief moment. Each failed relationship was like another layer of plaster over her already rock hard heart. She held everyone at arm's length and couldn't receive help, advice or genuine love from another person. One night after a bad break up she told me she was afraid of being alone. She said if she wasn't in a relationship she felt like she was nobody. I walked through some dark days with her until she finally left town. My heart still breaks for her. What happened to her at age twelve now rules her life with an insecurity she's been unable to overcome. But healing is possible, as we'll soon discover.

A Pattern of Insecurity

While writing, researching and observing this behavior in others and myself, I began to notice a recurring theme in each person's struggle. Everyone's insecurity manifested itself differently—for me it was weight, for Silvia it was negativity, for Travis the constant need for approval and Sherri the inability to love herself— but always seemed to follow the same pattern:

The person has no real sense of identity,

which makes it easy to believe lies,

leading to an unrealistic fear of what other people think.

Remember the definition of insecurity: *not confident or sure, uncertain, not adequately guarded or sustained, not firmly fastened or fixed.* I know this was definitely true in my own situation so I started a blog as an outlet to share my thoughts and discoveries with anyone who would read. About two years into it, I received this note from a woman:

My insecurity comes from something horrible that happened to me in the past. It wasn't even my fault. I was molested by someone in my family and I carry this weight around that I can't even explain. I'm scared to open myself up to anyone, and I can't seem to trust anyone, so I hold everyone at arm's length. I'm married but my husband doesn't understand how to handle me. I want to experience the love I see around me from other people but something holds me back. I want so badly to break free, but I don't know how. Anonymous .

She's not the only one crying out for help. Several others wrote their thoughts.

My struggle is self-image. This is a battle I'm so tired of. Caring too much about what other people think, feeling too fat and un-comfortable with looking fat in my clothes. Ugh! Eating right and exercising then feeling discouraged when the pounds don't melt away in 7 days. This seems minimal compared to the world's very real problems but very real in my daily walk. Suzi .

My insecurity was created by a family member who told me that what I wanted so badly in life wasn't a good idea and that I had to figure something else out because I'd never "make a living" at it. When you're a child, you are taught to believe what adults tell you...so I'd given up my dream. Heather.

I struggle to overcome insecurity by competition. If I am better than the next guy, the majority of the class or even who I used to be then I feel a sense of security in my life, but it's not real and it does not last. It's an exhausting way to live. I'm trying to over-come it. Katie M.

I think my biggest insecurity is not being good enough. I tend to overcompensate in the areas I feel like I am failing. Shawna.

I display my insecurity in the need to control everything around me or in the extra weight I carry. I certainly feel like I have to prove myself ALL THE TIME. Mandy M.

I have an unhealthy fear of what other people think. I don't know how I got to this place or how to get out of it. Every time I walk into a room I think in the back of my head, what are people thinking about me? Are they talking about me? Do they think I'm dressed right? Do I look like I fit in? I hate this about myself, but I don't know how to stop. Vickie.

Anna, I keyed in breaking free from insecurity and you're the first site that popped up. I know this is God! I'm so tired of this sickness ruling my life. I am a wife of a Bishop and after a 15-year relationship my husband wants to leave me because of the damage my insecurities have done to him and our family. I'm asking God to show me how to get free. Anonymous

Frankly, I could just scream when I think how we let insecurity ruin the most sacred relationships in our lives, let it keep us from loving freely, from accomplishing our dreams, from the amazing life God designed for us. He says in his word that He has come that we may have life and have it abundantly. (John 10:10) Living in insecurity is NOT the life He chose for us. He did not bleed and suffer so we could be held back by the fear of what other people think. He did not die on the cross so we could be kept from our full potential. This world needs us to be who we really are. We cannot live in the suffocating air of insecurity any longer, slaves to worry, fear, or doubt. We must find a way out of this mess. If we don't, we risk passing our insecurities to our children, we risk losing the battle of sin in our lives, we risk dragging the name of Jesus in the mud because we can't get past our own self-doubt and self-destruction. God might be calling us to do something that will never get done because of our insecurity and doubt. In Ephesians chapter 1 Paul writes that if we are followers of Christ, we have the same power within us that raised Christ from the dead. The same power. If that is true, why aren't we living our life as if that power resides within us?

I know what it is like to live in those chains and I know what it is like to live in freedom. Freedom is better by far. I want to share with you the things God has revealed to me. I want to invite you into the pain of my own past so that maybe God can use it to change the course some of us are on. I cannot tell you that it will be easy; some of the things we are going to talk about will be painful. But I can tell you if you will make a commitment to be honest with yourself, dig deep into those forgotten places of your heart, and open yourself to the possibility of freedom, you will find it.

Insecurity, beware. We're coming after you.

Take a deeper step: In_Security

1. Choose an area of focus. What is that one big insecurity you want to overcome?

Feeling like I am overlooked by others. Feeling uninvited

2. Think about the relationships in your life and write down the names of three individuals you trust and admire who love and follow Jesus. These will be your believers!

Adonis
Jessica
PJ

3. Stop right now and send these individuals a text, email or phone call asking them to help you on this journey of freedom.

Three

Pigs in the Pen

I mentioned earlier that I grew up in a family with seven children, all from the same mom and dad with a sixteen year span between first and last. My mom jokes that she's been pregnant for over five years of her life and if you've been pregnant even once, you know what kind of sacrifice that requires from your body. Another sacrifice my parents made as we were growing up was to educate us at home — every single one of us. Now before you let your minds go too far I have to tell you we were not the stereotypical home schooled family with no social skills, wearing matching denim jumpers and tennis shoes. We didn't churn our own butter, or milk our own cows. We were what I like to call sort-of normal.

Living with six other brothers and sisters made for an interesting upbringing. I was definitely never alone and seldom knew privacy. We were and still are a close-knit family. We learned a lot about getting along with others because there was plenty of opportunity to learn it.

I can remember more than once after our school was done for the day, Mom would order everyone outside so she could have a little peace and quiet. (With two small children of my own now, I look back and wonder how she did it with seven!) The warm sunny days were the best. Barefoot, we would tumble out to the front yard and choose any number of games to keep us occupied. One of our favorites was Pigs in the Pen. The person playing "it" was the wolf and his job was to try and catch all the pigs and send them to the pen. Basically, Tag. The difference was that the pigs could tag each other out of the pen if they could get close enough without getting caught themselves. Yes, I played a pig most of the time and knowing my weight was a sensitive issue, my brothers and sisters loved to point out that fact. (Who said home schooling saved you from being bullied?)

It was fun, unless of course, you got caught and had to sit in the pen. That happened to me a lot, being a slow runner and not very athletic. I'd try to cheat, claiming the wolf never touched me, but eventually I would have to give in, stomp to the pen, sit on the ground with my arms crossed and just wait hoping someone would tag me out of jail. There's nothing worse than being stuck in jail.

What is Insecurity?

When I think about insecurity I'm reminded of the hopeless feeling I had as a girl stuck in the pen, except this time I didn't have anyone who could tag me out. It was a personal prison of insecurity that I allowed to grow up around me, isolating myself from others, believing the lie that I was alone. I think so many people who struggle with insecurity find themselves in the same situation. We are confined in an indefinable, invisible prison with no one to help us out. From the outside we look normal. We try to smile, try to act the part, try to fit in... but inside we are worried, timid, frightened that at any moment someone might see behind the mask.

When I was first trying to discover the real source of my problem, I needed to define what it was I was truly fighting. So I began asking myself, what is insecurity? What is it really? I know it's a word used to describe a certain way of feeling but what *is* it? Over the course of several weeks and many journal entries I finally came to the conclusion that insecurity is bondage.

Bondage is any thought or action that limits our freedom. Insecurity creates a prison built of our own self-doubt, and barred with our own fears. It is a very real and tangible bondage and yet it can be indefinable and sometimes feel near-ly impossible to defeat, like invisible shackles on the ankles and wrists of our inner being, capturing and holding us hostage, just like the pigs in the pen.

That picture from my childhood is exactly how I felt insecurity play out in my life. That pen represented more than just a childhood memory. It represented my bondage. Every time I gave in to an insecure thought, or allowed my fear to keep me down, it was like locking myself in a prison, walls made of fear, bars held in place by deception. I was paralyzed with no ability to move forward.

These invisible bars are cast from many things: past failures, addictions, verbal, emotional or physical abuse, fear, pride. People we work with, people we live with, people we pass on the street, maybe even the person we see in the mirror struggle under the weight of this bondage, unable, unwilling or un-knowing how to break free. But it doesn't have to be that way.

So above all, insecurity is bondage. But what else is it? Through my own journey and research I've come to understand insecu-rity better through the following descriptions:

An inner stronghold that projects an outward struggle

Have you ever seen those old photo slides where the pictures in the slides are about a one-by-one square, but shown through a projector they are much bigger on the screen? Insecurity is a lot like those little pictures, filed away inside us where we think maybe if we're good enough at hiding them no one will ever know what's going on. Our heart is like the slide projector, and anytime the pressure is on or we find ourselves outside our comfort zone the insecurity shows itself much bigger on the outward screen of our lives.

Although the core issue is the same, each person's insecurity projects a different picture. The difference in the way it shows on the outside has a lot to do with each individual's upbringing, philosophy of life, personality type and life experience. Think for a moment how your insecurity might outwardly reveal itself. Do you shrink back in fear, passing yourself off as shy? Do you feel like you always need to fill a silent moment, coming off as very talkative, even obnoxious? Are you critical of others, even yourself? Do you judge yourself or other people too harshly? Are you fearful of people getting to know the real you? Do you dislike something about yourself and so isolate yourself from the love and acceptance of others because you cannot accept yourself? What about people you work with or interact with on a regular basis? Could some of their behaviors be tied to their insecurities?

I have a good friend I'm helping walk through her journey to freedom as I write this chapter. Each time we sit down to talk she compares herself to other people. She complains she's not as pretty as this girl, or as bold as that one. She'll never be what this person is, or never accomplish what another has done. Whatever insecurity she's facing shows itself in her constant need to compare. What about you? Have you thought through some of your past interactions? Think about the times when you felt like there was pressure on you or when you were the most uncomfortable.

Comparison

As you continue to read, it is important that you begin to identify what insecurity you may battle. I hope you will start writing down some thoughts or past experiences that come to mind to begin your own journey toward freedom.

A cycle

Another thing we must understand is that insecurity can be a deadly cycle. It might start out small. A seemingly insignificant bad habit or tendency that trips you up, but left unchecked only grows bigger and deeper over time. Remember I said earlier that my weight was a big insecurity but the only thing that made me feel better about it was to eat? The thing that made me insecure was the very thing I kept feeding. The more insecure I felt, the more I would self-medicate with food. I was on a vicious cycle with no idea how to stop it. People who aren't consciously fighting to overcome their insecurities might actually be feeding their insecurities unaware.

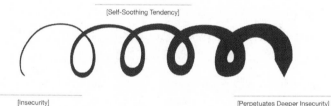

[Self-Soothing Tendency]

[Insecurity]　　　　　　　　　　　　　　　[Perpetuates Deeper Insecurity]

Another bright, beautiful young woman with great potential admitted that she is so insecure she feels she has to fill any silence with talking. I found it interesting that she knew this about herself, and yet didn't do anything to stop it. She so feared being alone that she would continue a conversation well past the norm just so she didn't have to be alone. The sad thing is, the more she fed her insecurity the more people didn't want to be around her.

What about you? What insecurity are you facing? Perhaps you are insecure about asking people for help. You may think if you ask for help you will be a burden to others, or that it may be a sign of weakness to ask for help, so you do everything on your own, and if others do try to help, you end up pushing them away because you insist on doing it yourself.

Maybe you are overly critical of others because you don't feel good about yourself. You think putting others down will make you feel better, and if you can get others to agree with your critical behavior you have won even more. But what you might not be aware of is that every time you say a negative word about someone else you are tossing your insecurity a T-bone steak. It might make you feel better for a brief moment, but deep down you are only making that monster stronger.

My friend Silvia is a perfect example of this. As each year passes with more disappointments she becomes more cynical and negative, which only seems to push men away and keep her in her stronghold cycle of doubt, a snowball becoming an avalanche.

This cycle can also be like digging yourself into a hole, like Sherri, the girl with a new relationship every month. There she is with an imaginary shovel in hand, and each time she decides to give in to her insecurity and jump into another dead-end relationship, she digs a little deeper. Since that relationship didn't work out she tries another. By now the cycle is a comfort zone. This is all she's ever really known, so trying something different seems foreign. Another attempt to fill the emptiness inside and she's dug herself into an impossible situation with no idea how to get out.

On and on it goes, the deadly cycle of insecurity. Each time we choose to allow our insecurity to control our behavior, we bind ourselves tighter and dig our holes deeper, until we look up and realize we're not the people we want to be. So we need to ask ourselves what will happen if we continue on this path? What insecurities are we feeding without even knowing? The quicker we realize we're on a deadly cycle the quicker we'll be able to end it.

Self-centered

selfishness

Insecurity is deceiving. People struggle every day but may be blind to the fact that insecurity is what really holds them back. And its source? Self-centeredness. Insecurity is selfishness to the core. Let me give you few examples.

Remember the insecure thoughts going through my head while I was waiting to be chosen for that ultimate Frisbee game? *I'm no good at sports. They probably wish I wasn't even here. I'll make us lose. I should sit out.* What is the focus of each of those sentences? I. I. I. I. I. All I was ever concerned about

45

was me. I was the most important person in my mind and I never thought much about others, except to worry what they thought of me.

What do your insecure thoughts sound like? Who is the main subject of the thoughts going through your head? It's okay, I've thought them all too. *What do people think about me? I'm no good. I'll never amount to anything. My life is a waste. I'm not as good as so-and-so. Do I fit in? Am I worth it?* Insecure thoughts don't have to just be self-degrading thoughts either. Pride, cynicism, comparison or negativity—anytime we allow insecure thoughts to control our minds, we are being self-centered.

Whatever insecurity we face grows from selfish thinking. We were born that way. It is hard-wired into our sin nature, but we can't leave it that way. We have to understand that the enemy wants us to stay selfish. He wants us to be self-thinking, self-centered and self-sabotaging individuals. He knows if he can keep us there we'll never find the keys to unlock the chains of insecurity that keep us bound.

Pride

We have seen how insecurity is selfish, but what if I told you that insecurity is also pride? "Now, hang on," you might say. "You are saying insecurity is pride? I'm not prideful. I have a poor self-image. There's no way I'm prideful." But I have come to understand this statement as a truth in my life:

Any preoccupation with SELF is pride.

Read that again. Whether our self-image is puffed up or deflated, if we are focusing on ourselves we are prideful. We assume that we have the right to set the standards, even for ourselves. When we are preoccupied with ourselves, how we fit in, how we look, how we compare to others, we often set that worry above God. God hates pride because it takes His rightful place as first in our lives. So whether we struggle with not believing in ourselves or believing in ourselves too highly, when all we ever think about is ourselves, we are being prideful.

Sin

When we allow our flesh to have full reign over our thoughts and emotions we are allowing the enemy a foothold into our lives. Unguarded thoughts are dangerous. They can lead us to dark places; they can lead us to actions we would never do in our right mind. When we don't know or believe in who God has created us to be, we inadvertently believe that God's creation is not all that the Bible says it is. We sell ourselves short and at the same time sell Him short as well. Insecurity is a sin, and though we may not realize it, when we give in to insecure thoughts, we are giving into a sin that can leave us mentally, emotionally and spiritually crippled.

One of the most painful memories of my past insecurities had to do with a man in my life. I liked him a lot. I had an unhealthy emotional attachment to him and would foolishly allow his attention to control my emotions. If he wanted to see me, I was the happiest person alive. If he gave me the cold shoulder, I might as well have been dead for all the life I showed. He led me on and I allowed it. My emotions were his puppet, and though he might not have known it, he had a power over me that was so destructive I'm still healing from it today. I was no longer living my life for me, or God or anyone else. I was living for him, living for his attention, his affection and his validation. I allowed my identity to be wrapped up in who I was to him, and when he could not reciprocate the feelings it was one more indication that I was undesirable and rejected.

I thank God I was able to get out of that sinful trap. It was not that he was a bad person, it was that I allowed myself to find my worth in him, a person going through his own struggles who couldn't possibly give me what I needed. Though it was one of the most painful experiences of my life, and a season of brokenness that left me forever changed, I think God allowed me to go through it to continue my transformation. He wanted me to realize that nothing, not one thing in this world, would ever satisfy me like He could. I was made by Him and for Him and until I realized this, every person, thing, or circumstance left me empty. The same is true for you. Insecurity will always hold us back from being the person God designed us to be. The good news is that we do not have to live in this bondage any longer. Freedom can be ours if we are willing to fight for it every day. And fight we will.

Take a deeper step: In_Security

1. What do you believe is an inner stronghold in your life? Where do you feel trapped or held back?

2. What ways do you see this stronghold projecting outwardly in your life?

3. Using the cycle diagram from page 43, write out your own cycle of how you might be feeding your insecurity without realizing it.

Four

Here's Your Sign

We've been talking pretty seriously over the last few chapters. Let's have a little fun and play a game called, "You Might Be Insecure If." Over the years I've had the opportunity to observe insecurity in many forms and stages, and have compiled a list of some signs of insecurity to help us continue to become students of our own behavior. As you read, see if you can identify the presence of an insecurity you may battle in your life. Once an illness is diagnosed it is much easier to know what treatment to apply to fight it off. The same is true in this case. Knowing the battle we fight gives us a better advantage in winning it.

Taking things too personally You might be insecure if you take things too personally. Co-workers, family, even friends feel they can't joke around with people like this because their feelings are bound to get hurt. They're wound too tightly and take themselves too seriously. Most of the time they're overly sensitive to what people say, and are easily offended. Any kind of constructive criticism feels like the end of the world.

Defensive You might be insecure if you're always defensive. People who are defensive do not feel safe in who they are. They have a difficult time being honest with themselves and others for fear of rejection or losing a place of status. They may exaggerate the details in situations to make themselves look like they are coming out on top. They rationalize, justify, and blame anyone but themselves. They need to feel they have an answer for everything, and generally exude a strong sense of pride. Being defensive means protecting themselves against anything and everything that threatens who they think they are or how they want to appear to others. Defensive people want to be right all the time and even when they are not, don't want to admit it. They are usually more talk than action, believing if they paint a good picture, no one will really know what's going on underneath.

Over Explaining You might be insecure if you are an over-explainer. People who over explain generally offer unsolicited information due to a perceived judgment from other people. A woman with an angry toddler in the grocery store caught my eye the other day. I assumed her daughter was wailing about something she couldn't have. As I passed, the woman shrugged her shoulders and said something about her daughter missing her nap. We've all been there. Maybe not with a fussy toddler, but we explain things to complete strangers because we think we can control their opinion of us.

Difficult time showing genuine care for others You might be insecure if you have a difficult time showing genuine care for others. This one may shock some of us, but the truth is, our insecurity can keep us from showing genuine care for others because we're too afraid to offer help. What might happen if I offer help and it doesn't work? What if I get caught up in something I don't want to do? What will other people think if I try to help?

I didn't think of this as a sign of insecurity until I caught myself thinking those exact thoughts. A homeless woman walked into the coffee shop where I was writing a couple weeks ago. She was loud and seemed not quite all there mentally. She kept yelling out and asking people for money. I caught the eyes of many other patrons and we all had the same look. Now, I don't think I'm a bad person but something kept me from reaching out to this woman. Maybe it was laziness, maybe it was the thought that the manager of the store needed to take care of her, but when I started to realize the thoughts going through my head I understood that it was insecurity that kept me from showing genuine Christlike care for this woman. "I don't want to help this woman, because everyone is watching her and if I help, then everyone will be watching me." How stupid. I feel kind of silly just sharing that. I cared more about what other people thought than about helping a poor woman who needed a hand.

The Need to Control You might be insecure if you constantly feel the need to control. A sense of control can be a security blanket. If we think we're in control, we feel better about a situation. If we know we're not in control, we will do anything to try to get it back.

A woman I once knew was so controlling she repelled everyone around her. Her children were the main objects, but her controlling nature generally found a way to overflow into the other relationships around her as well. As a successful businesswoman she used the thing she felt would bring her the most security: money. She used money to control her children, her friends, friends of her children, and anyone else she felt like she needed to control. This woman never smiled. She was so afraid of losing control she couldn't even enjoy the life she was living.

Early in my marriage I noticed I would often use my emotions to try to control my husband. I quickly found out he wasn't falling for my covert manipulation. When I realized this was ultimately a sign of insecurity, I had to do some soul searching. Why did I feel the need to control? I discovered my desire to control came out of fear.

Threatened You might be insecure if you feel threatened by those around you. I am not talking about the feeling you might get if someone were to threaten your life or safety, but about the more subtle kind of threat that awakens our insecurities.

At a graduation party a couple months ago I sat on the couch visiting with some friends when a couple of high school girls walked into the room. These girls were gorgeous — blonde, tan, perfect bodies and stylishly dressed. They came to sit on the same couch and immediately I felt threatened. In my eyes I didn't measure up to these girls. I had 15 pounds on them and I was wearing a Walmart dress! I compared myself to them and in my eyes, I didn't measure up to such beauty.

What about things other than beauty? I knew a man once who seemed to have the Midas touch; almost everything he did was successful. He was a brilliant leader, but because they didn't understand the gift he had, many of his colleagues appeared threatened by the fact that he was a better leader than they. Often they would talk badly about him, putting him down, seemingly to make themselves feel better. (I thought that kind of stuff ended in high school?) Instead of learning from him, they let their own insecurities control their thinking and keep them bound.

Constant Apologies You might be insecure if you constantly apologize for everything. This sign of insecurity can be so subtle that many people don't realize they are slaves to it. Apologizing is an important social skill. Knowing how to properly apologize when you have wronged someone is good, but I'm talking about the self-focused, excessive apologizing exhibited by victims of severe insecurity. A girl I met with a couple years ago struggled greatly with this very thing. She apologized for having me meet with her, she apologized for ordering her coffee before me, she apologized for not being able to pick out a place to sit. Once we started talking, she apologized for sharing too much, not saying the right thing, being too needy. She seemed to be apologizing for taking the time I spent with her. Maybe she didn't feel she was worth it, or she was just so self-conscious she needed the constant reassurance of others to help her get through life.

Being around someone who excessively apologizes for everything is exhausting! From my study of insecurity I've come to the conclusion that individuals who unreasonably apologize are looking for validation through responses such as, "Oh, it's okay." "You're fine." "Don't worry about it." This kind of response makes them feel less insecure about who they are or what they are doing, but it is a short-lived way to gain validation, which only causes a person to dive deeper into the deadly cycle of insecurity. Instead of finding their validation in something that lasts, they find it in something that's constantly changing, causing them to become validation junkies, looking for a fix anywhere they can get it.

Can't Take a Compliment You might be insecure if you can't take a compliment. Try this experiment the next time you go to work or spend time with a group of friends: give someone a compliment. It can be about anything from what they're wearing to the way their hair looks or how talented they are. It never fails, someone won't be able to receive a compliment. I see it as another sign of insecurity. Oftentimes people who can't take a compliment are doing one of two things — or both. Either they don't think anything about themselves is good enough to receive a compliment, or they defer the compliment so that the person giving it will just continue to give more. I used to engage in this behavior all the time. When I realized it rooted in insecurity I worked hard to start receiving compliments graciously.

Comparison and Jealousy You might be insecure if you compare yourself to others. One of the biggest sources of insecurity is comparison and the jealousy it breeds. I've heard it said that comparison kills contentment, and it's all too easy, especially in the world of social media, to find endless sources of discontent, because there will always be someone prettier, smarter, skinnier, more creative, and more popular than we, and even if we think otherwise there are countless things that we envy in others that have nothing to do with the outward appearance. I know I have been guilty of this. It is so hard to escape, and it is such a waste. Comparison and jealousy are deeply rooted in a discontentment and insecurity in ourselves. Only when we learn to love ourselves for who God created us to be, can we live free.

Judgment You might be insecure if you secretly (or perhaps not so secretly) judge others. The first time I noticed this manifestation of insecurity I was watching *What Not to Wear*, a fashion show on TLC, in which the hosts pretty ruthlessly go through someone's wardrobe and then help their guest find things to wear that are more flattering to their body type, age and personality. When they showed one of their guests an outfit they recommended, the girl's comment was, "I would never wear that!" They asked her why not and she replied, "I would be too afraid people would think, 'Look at her, she's trying to show off wearing those prints. Who does she think she is?'" The host asked her why she would think that, and the guest gave herself away in this one remark, "That's what I would think if I saw someone wearing that." Wow, I was shocked at this. This woman was holding herself back from something because of her own judgmental behavior toward other people. I began discussing this behavior with some of my friends and we laugh at how many times we have done the same. We do or don't do certain things because we fear being judged by others — because we ourselves judge others too harshly. "Do not judge so that you will not be judged. For in the way you judge, you will be judged; and by your standard of measure, it will be measured to you." Matthew 7:1, 2. If you struggle with being judgmental, it may be time for you to admit that you are dealing with insecurity.

False Humility

So far we've focused mainly on how our own insecurities affect us, but what about other people's insecurities? Do they affect us? Definitely. Whether you're working hard to lose weight, grow spiritually, better yourself materially, or pursue your dreams in any number of ways, there will be people who, because of their own insecurities, will try to undermine your efforts. Sometimes their actions will come disguised as good intentions on their part—efforts to save you from being too hard on yourself, from possible heartbreak, from possible or probable failure. People too insecure to pursue their own goals can find it all too easy to resent those who do. As Will Smith's character in *The Pursuit of Happyness* told his son, "You got a dream. You gotta protect it. People can't do something themselves, they wanna tell you you can't do it. If you want something, go get it. Period."

Likewise, if you're not careful, other people's insecurities can cause you to hold yourself back from doing or being your best. Maybe you sense that others feel threatened around you, so you don't feel like you can be yourself. Because of their insecurities, they may not understand your confidence or resolve, and so you hold yourself back to make them feel better. I call this a false humility. It does nothing to help either party. In the words of Nelson Mandela, "When you let your light shine, you unconsciously give others permission to do the same." When we are free to be ourselves, not caring what others think, and not shrinking back so others feel more comfortable around us, we encourage others to that same freedom. More about that in the coming chapters, but remember, the enemy wants nothing more than to keep us distracted by believing lies and caring what others think.

Take a deeper step: In_Security

1. Which sign of insecurity do you identify with the most? Do you struggle with a sign of insecurity that wasn't mentioned? What is it?

Jealousy + Comparison

2. What ways have you caught yourself acting out of this insecure behavior?

3. Write a few sentences to your insecurity as if you are leaving it for good.

Five

Welcome to the Circus

We lie — by omission, by overinflation of the truth, or by deliberate falsification. We lie to be nice. We lie to be mean. We lie to fit in. We lie to feel safe. We all have lied. The powerful feeling that can come with saying something other than the truth is equalled only by the anxiety that follows from the fact or possibility of being discovered. There is something powerful about the ability to make someone believe something other than the truth.

Have you ever been lied to? Whether you knew at the time or found out later, it can leave you shocked, appalled, or maybe even amused that a person could have the nerve to say something other than the truth. It can leave you feeling violated. Trust is broken. What else has this person lied about? Can I believe anything they say now? Doubt settles in. Whether it be a rebellious teenager lying about where they were or what they were doing, or a husband or wife hiding the truth, lies only end in pain and destruction.

The pain that comes from living in a lie is no different. So many of us are living in the middle of a lie and don't even know it. Do you ever wonder why you're not happier, why you seem to struggle with keeping your head above the current of life? Do you ever feel helpless or hopeless and find yourself seeking solace in things that only make you more miserable?

We have believed lies since the beginning of time. The serpent that deceived Adam and Eve, has been using lies to trip us up ever since. The father of lies uses his lies to steal the one thing he knows would give us power, if we just believed it: our identity. If he can effectively steal our identity we will fall for whatever charade he presents, whatever insecurity we allow to dominate our thoughts, words, and actions. And that is where so many of us find ourselves. Many of us don't even realize we are living in a lie. We have believed it for so long we have decided this is just how life is. So we give up, and make ourselves comfortable, getting farther and farther away from our true identity, the person God intended us to be when He created us.

We have already established that insecurity is bondage— bondage to believing lies. Our insecurities are simply the lies we have believed about ourselves our entire lives. The prison we lock ourselves in is made up of the lies we hold on to and the negative self-talk we indulge in, sometimes without being aware we are doing it. Where did these lies come from? Any number of sources could contribute to the lies we believe about ourselves. Maybe someone said something hurtful and it stuck with you. Maybe a parent told you they wished they never had you and you have carried that hurt and rejection around for years. Maybe your dad never accepted you. Maybe you have been told you are not smart enough, good enough, or pretty enough. Maybe an ex hurt you, so you believe no one can be trusted. Perhaps you have a vision or dream you'd like to accomplish, but the fear of failing always wins out.

In chapter two I mentioned a pattern of insecurity.

No real sense of identity,

which makes it easy to believe lies,

leading to an unrealistic fear of what people think.

No wonder the enemy wants to go after our identities. Everything we do flows from that source. It is where we need to start.

I read a story recently, about how elephants are trained for the circus. It really revealed to me how we have learned to live in our own lies. *"When young, [elephants] are attached by heavy*

65

chains to large stakes driven deep into the ground. They pull and yank and strain and struggle, but the chain is too strong, the stake too rooted. One day they give up, having learned that they cannot pull free. From that day forward they can be "chained" with a slender rope. When this enormous animal feels any resistance, though it has the strength to pull the whole circus tent over, it stops trying. Because it believes it cannot, it cannot."

When we believe a lie long enough, eventually we stop trying to break free. We give up, thinking, "This is just the way my life is going to be."

Perception and Reality

The striking thing about believing the lies that keep us in bondage is that we don't have to do it. We have the power to stop believing these lies, but we may not realize it. Like the elephant who is strong enough to pull over the whole tent, we have the ability to live free from the pain and heartache of believing lies, from bondage, from the negative opinions of others and even from the negative opinions we have of ourselves. But unfortunately if we don't know how, we continue our existence held back from all that God has in store for us.

So many people forget that they are responsible for their lives, that they are in control of their thinking and therefore they are responsible for the results or outcomes of the life God has given them. For too long I lived my life letting the lies dictate my actions, as if I was riding on the back of life, being jerked around by the relentless bucking instead of taking the reigns and guiding things in the right direction. For too long I have watched others succumb to lies never realizing how their own negativity created a reality in which they became lost. Why is this so important? Because our enemy, Satan, is not omniscient. He doesn't know our thoughts. He can only know what we tell or show him. That is why our words, actions, and therefore, our thoughts are so important. "For the mouth speaks what the heart is full of" (Luke 6:45).

If we believe a lie long enough, our words will reflect that lie, and pretty soon so will our actions. Eventually we will begin to believe the lie as truth, but a lie is, by definition, not true. When we talk about believing lies we must understand that our perception is, or can become, our reality. Our perception of ourselves, what we believe about ourselves, is the reality in which we will live. If we do not believe what we have to say matters, we won't speak up. If we do not think we can do something, we will likely not even try. If we do not believe in ourselves, if we have a poor self-image and hold ourselves back because of insecurity, we will act out of that perception and therefore it becomes reality. Because of this, people may doubt our ability, feel sorry for us, discount our credibility, or just not enjoy being around us.

Our words, actions and behaviors will follow whatever we believe about ourselves, and that's where the enemy gets a foothold. We teach others what to think about us by the way we think of ourselves. Our perception becomes our reality, so to change our reality we need to change our perception of who we are.

Lies Vs. Facts

Before going much further, we need to distinguish between a lie we believe about ourselves and a fact. I had to come to the realization that the lie about being fat was not actually a lie, it was a fact. I was fat. I weighed too much for my age and I was not living a healthy life. So, if that was true, what was the lie? The lie I believed was, "I'm fat, therefore I'm not whole, I'm not a real person. I have nothing to offer the world because of the way I look. I'm a reject." That was the lie. That is what held me back. It was an assault on my identity, who I was and who God had created me to be. The resulting negative thoughts led me to live my life in a false reality that I created.

I was reading to my children the other day about Jesus being tempted in the desert. The strategy the enemy was using each time he spoke with Jesus struck me as I read. He said, "If you are the Son of God." He attacked Jesus' identity, attempting to cast doubt on Who Jesus was and to Whom He belonged. Satan's tactics are no different for us. He will attack at our identity and if we don't have a firm grasp on who we are, and to Whom we belong, we will be vulnerable to his lies.

Everyone carries around a few lies they believe about themselves. Over the years I've collected some of the most common ones. Over the next few chapters, try to distinguish between the lie and the fact. The lie will always steal your identity.

Six

Lies that Steal a Woman's Identity

I'm nobody until somebody loves me No, it's not just an old love song. Unfortunately, it is a lie many people believe. I lived most of my single years with this kind of mindset. I thought that life didn't actually start until I had found the right man and married him. This lie is so ingrained in our society that even my grandmother, pulling me aside at my wedding rehearsal dinner, said, "Now your life has really begun." I know many single ladies who have bought into this lie. In the back of their minds they have that niggling thought, "Well, I'll just put this off until I'm married. I'll just put off getting into shape. I'll just put off starting my career. I'll just put off starting that ministry. I'll just put these things off until my life has really begun." Maybe you have been married before and you struggle with believing the lie that you are used goods and you fear you may never find anyone who wants to marry a divorcee. You're allowing your past to define who you are and giving the enemy fuel for the fire.

Single ladies aren't the only ones who struggle with this lie. I have met with married women who admit, with fear in their eyes, that they don't know what they would do if their husbands left them. Their identities are so wrapped up in their husbands that even the slightest argument sends them spiraling in fear and doubt about their relationship. Why? Because we believe we're nobody until somebody loves us.

The fact may be that you are still single, that your marriage ended in divorce, or even that you are in a loveless marriage. But the lie is that you are nobody, you have no life, you are undesirable. What horrible, self-degrading things to believe about ourselves! By believing such lies we are saying to the world that our worth, our significance, our identity is left up to the fickle mind of another human being. We are too valuable to believe such a thing.

Believing lies like this can do much damage to ourselves and even those closest to us. Remember the woman from chapter one who shared on my blog about how her insecurity has damaged her marriage of 15 years? My guess is that her identity is wrapped up in a lie a lot like this one. We don't realize what kind of pressure it puts on a man when we are trying to find our identity in him. I want to talk a little more about this lie, because as women we often identify ourselves based on the relationships we have—or don't have. It really is one of the biggest lies we face when it comes to our identity.

I know we have talked a lot about how our insecurity holds us back. But consider for a moment that your insecurity might also hold back your husband. Even if you are not yet married, stay with me. The old "ball and chain" might not be marriage itself, but marriage to a woman who is insecure. Here are three examples:

1. Perhaps your husband works with attractive women. If you are insecure, soon you are likely to say something. At first, it might be a passing comment to see if he's noticed the women in his office, but if your nagging insecurities are not satisfied by his response, your conversations or accusations might get much worse.

2. You might struggle with financial insecurity. No matter how much you have it never seems to be enough. Your unsettled distrust of God's provision for your family weighs heavily on your husband. Whether you contribute to the family finances with a second income or not, your husband is hardwired with the drive to provide for you. Even if you think you're good at hiding this distrust, it seeps out in ways of which you are unaware.

3. Insecurity in our body image is the perfect place for the enemy to put a wedge between a husband and his wife. You may avoid intimacy because you do not like the way you look or feel. After a while this avoidance can cause confusion, hesitation, and resentment in your relationship.

Let me talk briefly to single readers. Your insecurity may be holding back your husband as well. I understand about God's perfect timing. Bringing Mr. Right along should be out of your hands and firmly placed in God's. But ask yourself this question: Might God be waiting on *me* to learn a few things first? This was true in my own life. My insecurities were definitely holding back that beautiful moment when I first met my husband. I was not ready to be in a relationship because I had not yet found contentment in who I was as a single woman. I thought I would be happy once I was married. I had to find contentment and rest in the life I had, before God brought me my husband. And I'm sure glad I did. Discovering who I was, and loving myself for me before I entered into marriage has only served to strengthen the covenant I now share with my husband.

I have nothing to offer unless I'm young, thin and beautiful
This lie has many women addicted to the gym or the latest weight-loss diet. It has their wallets stretched thin from the latest beauty products, fashions and trends, all promising to keep them looking young and beautiful. It encourages women

to seek medical advice about the shape of their nose, the wrinkles on their foreheads, or the size of their stomach. Its deception keeps our noses in magazines and our eyes on what the world tells us is the standard of beauty. Image is everything these days. Too many people have bought into the lie that they are going to be overlooked or disregarded, or that they have nothing to offer unless they look a certain way. Keeping up with the world's standard of image and beauty feels like a never-ending treadmill.

I'm not opposed to being smart. Taking care of our bodies is important. Making ourselves look beautiful is part of the fun of being a woman. The problem comes when we allow this lie to steal our identity. I have nothing to offer unless I'm young, thin, and beautiful.

Beautiful to whom? To your husband? To your friends, co-workers, parents, siblings, or strangers? Who are we asking to answer this question? Are they giving us the answers we want? Are they satisfying our need for validation in the area of our image? What are we using as a measuring stick? What is our standard of beauty? Why do we continue to strive for beauty, and yet every time we look in the mirror we see the same old thing? Maybe because we are letting the wrong people decide what the standard of beauty should be. Have you ever asked yourself if *you* think you are beautiful? What did you say and why? It is no surprise that the enemy comes after us in the area of our image. Why not come after us there? So much of what we do comes directly from the way we feel about ourselves. He knows this about women. If he can get us down about how we look and feel about ourselves, he has the key to every other area of our lives.

The fact may be that you have a pimple on your forehead, or you carry too much weight, or wrinkles are settling in, but the lie is that you are therefore ugly and have nothing to offer the world. We must come to rest with who we are before we can look in the mirror and actually believe that we are beautiful. Maybe the reflection of the mirror is not where we begin. Maybe a better question to ask ourselves is, "What is the reflection of my heart? Have I accepted myself for who God made me to be? Am I acting beautiful?" Sometimes we have to act ourselves into a new way of thinking instead of thinking ourselves into a new way of acting. Until we begin to feel beautiful on the inside there is no amount of primping, prepping or plucking that can make us feel beautiful on the outside.

I'm not good enough unless I'm as strong and as successful as a man Society has caused many women to buy into this lie. We believe we have to be ruthless, cutthroat and sometimes heartless in our approach to our success. How else are we going to make it in this world run by men?

I struggled with this lie when I worked on staff at Life.Church, allowing it to distort who I was. I began to deny my heart as a woman and ultimately became someone I was never supposed to be. There was a season during which, I'll admit, I was a fake, trying too hard to make myself stand out, trying too hard to cover up the fact that I am a woman. Why? Because I believed the lies that women can't handle the same things men can, women are weaker than men, women are too emotional to handle things.

So I began to compete, trampling over the people I worked with instead of helping, nurturing and encouraging them, which is what I really wanted to do. I made my heart numb to the heartache I encountered in my job so that I wouldn't have the urge to cry. I even started dressing less femininely just so the men I worked with couldn't poke fun at me for being a girl. The problem was, the more I became something I wasn't, the less strength and power I actually had. The more energy I used trying to cover up who I was, the more I actually made those lies a reality. Remember, our perception becomes our reality.

Recognizing this lie has helped me realize my identity is not found in how well I can compete with the men around me, but in who I am, and accepting this has catapulted my influence and recharged my confidence. I believe that understanding we have been given tremendous strength in who we are, regardless of gender, is what will make us stand out. Instead of trying to hide our femininity, we need to learn to embrace it and work from the strength that our identity brings us. A woman at rest in who she is is a powerful thing. A woman secure in who God has created her to be is a weapon in His armory, perfectly poised to handle the challenges the enemy throws her way. It is time we take back our identity, quit believing the lie, and live from the strength that our uniqueness brings.

I'm nobody unless I'm better than somebody else This is the comparison lie. Sometimes it creeps into our thoughts when we meet someone new. We size the person up, taking in what she is wearing, how much makeup she has on, what he says, what he does for a living, how he acts, all the while trying to answer the unspoken questions, "Am I better than she? Am I more successful than he? Am I prettier? Do I dress better? How do I measure up against him?" I used to struggle with this lie more than I would like to admit. Thinking back on it now I realize it was because I was not secure in myself. I was always seeking that next thing that could make me feel good about myself. If it was at the expense of another person, it didn't really matter.

It hurts my heart to know that many men and women struggle with this need to compare. The scary truth is that other people are not our standard for living. So comparing ourselves to someone else is not only a waste of time, it is foolishness. Paul talks about this in 2 Corinthians 10:12 when he says, "When they measure themselves by themselves and compare themselves with themselves, they are without understanding." It is often the reason our encounters with each other, especially among women, can be so catty. It is definitely the reason I hate going to bridal and baby showers where the room is thick with the tension of comparison. It hurts me to know the reason we succumb to this form of interaction is because of our own insecurity. We believe our identity is wrapped up in how we measure up to others, and so we allow where we perceive ourselves to fall on this self-imposed measuring stick to decide how we feel about ourselves.

The fact may be another woman is prettier than you. The fact may be she has more money, more kids (or fewer kids) a bigger house, a better husband. But the lie comes when we use other people as a measuring stick for ourselves. No one, absolutely no one, has the power to tell us who we are and are not. That job is left to the One who created us. Who better to tell us who we are and how we measure up than the One who knew from the beginning what He was doing when He made us? We must recognize the comparison lie for what it is: an assault on our identity that should have no place in our thinking.

Seven

Lies that steal a man's identity

Women are not the only ones who struggle with insecurity and believing lies. I asked a number of men to share with me the top three or four lies they believe. The following are not all the ones they shared with me, but I feel they are a good representation of the lies men face today. And ladies, don't overlook this section. Sadly, in our gender-confused, role-reversed culture, these lies often ensnare women too.

I'm a failure Whenever I host a bridal shower I have the groom make a video of a few thoughts about himself. One question I ask the man is: "What is your greatest fear?" Every man I've ever interviewed came back with the same answer. Failure.

Oftentimes, if there is a chance of failure in trying something new, many men will not even give it a second look. They would rather pass up an opportunity than try and fail. But the outcome of our actions, whether success or failure, does not determine who we are.

I will never forget watching my older brother, Andrew, go through his divorce. He had been married for six years and had two beautiful daughters. One day his wife decided she was done. He fought and fought for her and their marriage but she had made up her mind. The divorce was lengthy and painful. Andrew carried around a weight that seemed impossible. During that very difficult time I noticed something about him. Though he had a failed marriage, he fought against the urge to internalize the failure. He fought to reject the lie that *he* was a failure just because his circumstances pointed him there. Though it was tough, some days nearly impossible, he continued to rejected the lie that he was a failure. He was only able to do this because of the strength he found in his relationship with Jesus Christ. Rejecting this lie enabled Andrew to overcome the fear and depression that came from the pain of his divorce. He says that after facing that dark time he believes there is nothing that he cannot overcome, but he had to realize that his identity is not found in his circumstances. Andrew is now married to a remarkable woman with whom he has three additional children. God redeems.

I think many men struggle with believing this lie. Perhaps they tried something and it failed and now, believing they are failures, they are afraid to take another risk. But what is the fact and what is the lie? The fact may be that you have a failed marriage. The fact may be that your bank account is in the red or that you got laid off. The fact may be that some of your circumstances are failing, but the lie is that *you* are a failure. You are not a failure. Failure is an event. Failure is never a person.

I am what I do Many men's identity is wrapped up in what they do for a living. Have you ever noticed when we meet someone new one of the first things we ask is, "What do you do?" Our society has taught us to buy into the lie that "I am what I do."

When my husband, Cody, and I first started dating, he didn't have a job. As a former Marine it took him a while to settle back into society and find work that suited his training, skills, and passions. There was not much call in the United States for a man to carry a rifle around and storm into abandoned buildings hoping to catch a few insurgents. He did odd jobs for a while and worked for his brother-in-law doing landscaping. But there was a period of about three months that he did not have any job. He carried this heavily.

One evening when he came to see me he seemed depressed. I asked him what was wrong and with a deep sigh he told me, "I need to find work." Since we have been married he has told me he was afraid of losing me because he didn't have a job. He thought I would not want to be with a "bum." He equated the fact that he didn't have a job with who he was. I knew I loved him when I found myself saying, "I don't care what you do. You could flip burgers at McDonalds for all I care. To me, who you are is not what you do."

Since that time, Cody has found a good job and loves what he does. I think it took him realizing that what he does for a living is not who he is as a man. Not allowing himself to be a victim of this lie has enabled him to take risks in his job that have advanced him in the company. What he does is not who he is. Who he is drives what he does and he is pretty darn good at it, if you ask me.

The fact may be that you do not have a job. The fact may be that you feel like you are stuck in a dead-end job that you hate. But the lie is that you are what you do. This lie is stealing your sense of value. The sooner we realize this lie for what it is, the sooner we will find our true selves and work from the strength it brings.

I'm Not Man Enough In his book *Wild at Heart*, John Eldridge says it perfectly, "…every man's deepest fear is to be exposed, to be found out, to be discovered as an imposter, and not really a man." He goes on to say that every man carries a wound. "Every boy, in his journey to become a man, takes an arrow in the center of his heart, in the place of his strength. Because the wound is rarely discussed and even more rarely healed, every man carries a wound. And the wound is nearly always given by his father."

This lie that many men believe is very closely related to the wound Eldridge is talking about. Many of our insecurities can come from believing lies that are inflicted on us by a parent. Many men are being held back from their full potential because they do not know how to overcome this lie and find healing for their wound. I highly recommend *Wild at Heart* because it takes an in-depth look at the heart of a man.

One of our friends recently opened up about some of his insecurities, showing that the lies he believes about himself come from that missing link to his father. "My father never really accepted me as a man, and because I never got the confirmation I needed, I'm constantly harder on myself than I need to be. It's really easy for the enemy to expose that insecurity in me when I actually do fail at something."

Many insecurities are born out of the lie that "I'm not man enough," which is so easy to believe, and causes men to hold themselves back from what God is calling them to do. The lie has robbed them of their identity. The first step to freedom from these lies is to admit to believing them. Not having a firm grasp on where one's identity comes from can be why fights with wives happen, why gambling and pornography are such huge addictions. Men struggle to find their strength and sense of self in something other than Christ, because they believe a lie and don't even realize it.

What We Must Do

I'll never amount to anything. I'm not smart enough. I'm a loser. I'm not beautiful. I'm not man enough. I have no purpose. I'm a failure. I'm the reason our marriage broke up. I'm worthless. I'm dirty. I can't do it. I'm fat. I have nothing to live for.

The pain that comes from believing lies can be unbearable, yet, somehow the enemy has tricked us into living life locked in the chains of these lies. If we just knew how, if we just had the key to unlock the chain, we, like the circus elephants, would have the power to topple over the entire tent. We could break free from the chains and stakes that are holding us down.

I say it is time to declare war on these lies. It is time to get a little sweaty, get a little bloody, and use the weapons we have been given to fight this battle we all face. It is time to take back who we are and find the life of freedom we were meant to live. If you want that freedom, keep reading.

Take a deeper step: In_Security

1. What lie have you believed for so long it has become your reality? Explain.

2. Is there something about yourself that may be a fact but which you could change if you worked at it hard enough? What is it?

3. What keeps you from making that change?

Part 2

Presence

Perception

Power

Eight

You Are Here

The GPS app on my phone is one I use a lot. I love it. I know I can get anywhere I need to go, even if I've never been there before. I simply pull it up, plug in the address of my destination and watch it navigate the most efficient route for me to take. It makes me feel safer, looking down at the little blue dot that represents me, as it pulses with movement, showing me each turn to take. I know exactly where I am and exactly where I need to go because I have a satellite perspective that is above the winding streets and crazy traffic. Wouldn't that satellite perspective be a great thing for life as well—something that allowed us to look at ourselves from a different perspective and know exactly where we are in life and how far we have to go to get to the person we want to be? There is such a tool, but for many it can be difficult to find and even more difficult to use.

But for us to continue this battle of breaking free we need to learn what it is and how to harness the power it can bring us. The tool is self-awareness.

Self-Awareness

Having self-awareness is having a correct view of who you are. It is what is true about yourself. Self-awareness is the first step for all growth and development. You can't change or move forward until you first know where you are. One of the first places we can look for self-awareness is in the mirror. If you're not too lazy or too cool do me a favor and go look in the mirror right now. If you don't want to do it right now, do it the next time you're in the bathroom, or a place with a mirror. Go ahead. Look at your reflection. Stare at yourself. What do you see? Do you know who are you? What are your strengths and weaknesses? What type of personality do you have? Are you a rule follower or a free spirit? A lover or a fighter? Do you like who you are? What do you like? What do you not like? I'm not just talking about your appearance. What do you feel when you look at yourself? Do you feel shame? Depression? Joy? Are you proud of yourself or disappointed? Is it hard for you to look at yourself so intently? Are you able to be honest with yourself?

The reflection of a mirror is something we take for granted today. Back in the late 1200s glass manufacturers created a special group called The Glassmakers Guild for the purpose of safeguarding the secrets of the mirror-making trade and its profitability. Back then only royalty could afford to buy mirrors and historians say some nobles went so far as to sell their property to buy a beautifully made mirror. During that time mirrors were valued and sought after. Today, mirrors are everywhere. We don't think twice about the ability to see our reflection, but we may be missing an opportunity for our reflection to tell us something about ourselves. Looking at your reflection is a powerful thing. It gives you the chance to crawl out of your skin for a moment and consider the person before you in a more objective way. You might be surprised by what you discover from this exercise of introspection.

If we are not up to the task of taking a serious look in the mirror, our hopes of making lasting change in our lives will never become reality. But our reflection is only part of the picture. Self-awareness can be like trying to look at a framed picture from inside the frame. There is only so much we will be able to see about ourselves before blindspots in our growth for freedom become evident. We need an outside-the-frame perspective, a satellite perspective, to be able to see the whole picture. This is where the next part of self-awareness comes in.

Feedback

I love this definition of Newton's Law of Motion when thinking about feedback.

"An object either remains at rest or continues to move in the same direction unless acted upon by an external force."

You are that object, and if you want to change the course you are on and free yourself from your bondage to insecurity, you need an external force to help you get the momentum started. That external force is feedback.

Feedback can be scary, and unsolicited or unwanted feedback can be downright humiliating. But when it comes to self-awareness, getting feedback is simply reconciling what you know about yourself with what everyone else already knows about you. In other words, when gaining self-awareness, often-times, we are the last to know the things we need to do to help make us better. Wouldn't you rather be proactive in your approach to gaining feedback instead of reactive to the feedback that may come?

When I was a youth pastor I was immersed in a culture of feedback. Not one event was done without discussing later what did and didn't work and how we could do it better the next time. Being a part of a culture like that taught me three things.

1. **Develop a thick skin.** Nothing is worse than hearing you're missing the mark, you aren't your best, or you could do things better. It can be easy to take feedback personally and

allow its effects to send your belief in yourself into a downward spiral. That's why the second and third things I learned about feedback are so important.

2. **Feedback is meant to help you.** Most people when giving feedback only want what's best for you. True, some people like to pick things apart and seem to have the spiritual gift of nit-picking, but true feedback should always be life-giving and help you get to the next step in your development. If it's not, check out the next thing.

3. **Chew up the meat, spit out the bones.** This saying was a constant among our staff. It means that while all feedback can be helpful, focusing on too many things at once can be detrimental. Take the one or two big things that come out of someone's feedback and leave the rest behind.

You Asked For It

The world we live in is not prone to providing direct, life-giving feedback. People will talk all day long behind your back about what they think you could do to be better, but something keeps us from sharing that information with each other. Unwanted feedback is just that, unwanted. However, as embarrassing as it may be to have a stranger tell you there's spinach in your teeth, or a booger hanging out your nose, you're glad they told you before anyone else saw it. Recognizing our insecurities and hang-ups is the spinach-in-the-teeth kind of awareness we are after. Everyone has blindspots that hinder growth, and if you don't think you do, that may be your blindspot. But feedback in this area doesn't just come. You have to ask for it. You have to create in yourself a culture where feedback is valued and used to make you better. I'm not suggesting you invite every person you're associated with to give you feedback. Select two or three individuals whom you trust and admire (your believers) to be the ones to speak into your life. It could be your husband or mom, a mentor or pastor, an older sister or friend. When you have these people in mind explore these three steps to create a culture of feedback in your life.

Teach people how to give you feedback. Early in our marriage, Cody and I developed the habit of occasionally asking each other this question. "What is one thing I can do to be a better spouse?" We did this at an unemotional time when we could focus on each other and talk things through. Asking a question like this opens the door for constructive feedback. It shows the other we are open to change and desire to grow. Notice, we didn't ask, "Is there anything I do that annoys or makes you angry?" Keeping your question around one positive outcome helps guide the feedback from getting lost in the weeds or subjecting each other to a verbal firing line. Here are a few examples of great questions you could ask: "Do you see something in me that's holding me back from reaching the next step in my growth?" "Is there a blindspot in my life that's keeping me from being the person I'm created to be?" "Do you see an insecurity in me that's keeping me in bondage?" It's important they know you desire honesty, even if it may hurt at first.

Opening yourself to feedback is intimidating, but what you do with that feedback paves the road to true life-change.

Your response to feedback. If you have a negative response to someone's solicited feedback, they will not continue to help you. Becoming defensive, which is a sign of insecurity, and making up excuses for the answers someone gives you is the wrong response. If you have asked someone to speak into your life, listen respectfully, ask any follow-up questions to gain clarity, and use the new information to create a game-plan for change. This is what gaining self-awareness is all about. There is no need to feel embarrassed about the information you receive, even though you may feel embarrassed at first. Remember, the feedback you're getting was something already known by those around you and they still chose to love you. Now you know it too and you can take confident steps toward your development.

Baby Steps. Although your steps may be confident, growth and development take time. Don't be discouraged if things don't seem to change right away. Take your new-found awareness and put it to work for you. Don't allow embarrassment or negativity to suck you deeper into a pit of insecurity. Use this awareness as stepping stones to help rise you to a higher level of perspective over your life. And take one step at a time.

Coming into a deeper knowledge about ourselves will only help us on the journey to freedom. In Appendix A I've created a list of resources on the subject of self-awareness. I encourage you to select one or two to add to your reading list if you desire lasting change in this area.

Why Self-Awareness Matters

Don't forget, our enemy is ruthless in his strategy to "steal, kill and destroy." Some might think he'll use an aggressive approach with attacks that are clearly coming from a place of evil. But remember, he is deceptive above all else. His best strategy is not necessarily one that draws you deeper into sin, but one that keeps you stagnant, stale. Without self-awareness you will not be able to move forward and learn how to break free from your strongholds. Don't be surprised if you feel tempted to skip this step in your journey toward freedom. Your enemy wants to keep you from growth and development. He wants to hold you back. If he can't keep you sinning, he'll just keep you stunted.

Take a deeper step: In_Security

Answer these questions from your reflection exercise. If you didn't use the mirror before, do it now. It's important.

Who are you?

What are your strengths and weaknesses?

What type of personality do you have?

What do you like about yourself? List five things.

What do you not like? List three things.

What do you feel when you look at yourself?

Are you proud of yourself or disappointed? Why?

Is it hard for you to look at yourself so intently? Explain.

Are you able to be honest with yourself? Why or why not?

Nine

Paradigm Shift

I always knew I wanted to be a writer. At an early age I discovered how words could come together to express thoughts I didn't even realize I was thinking. It came naturally to me and flowed out of me, helping me process the tumultuous emotions of young adult life through journaling. Writing also gave me an outlet for my vivid imagination. When I was sixteen I wrote a twenty-chapter novel. Was it any good? At the time I thought it was gold, but looking back now, I had no idea what I was doing. I just knew I loved to write.

I wanted to know all there was to know about writing, so after graduating high school I enrolled in a two-year correspondence writing course. During those two years, I attended a few writers conferences to which I would bring my work and meet with other writers, editors and agents. I was eighteen when I attended my first conference, and so inexperienced I didn't even know what I didn't know. But I was there soaking up all the knowledge I could about the skill and business of writing. What I didn't know was that God was using this opportunity to reveal to me one of the keys that would unlock the chains of my insecurity.

At eighteen, I was probably at my highest weight. At well over two hundred pounds I didn't take to large crowds very easily. I remember the first morning of the conference; a fresh layer of snow covered the ground outside and sunlight pierced the floor-to-ceiling windows in the lobby of the hotel, casting square shadows on the carpet. Completely alone, I walked through the lobby into the ballroom and instantly was assaulted by all-too-familiar thoughts. *What are people thinking of me? Do they think I'm fat? Can they tell I have no idea what I'm doing? Am I dressed right? Do I fit in?*

My first instinct was to run in the opposite direction, hop on the elevator and go back to my room where it was safe. I could not get past those thoughts. On and on they went. I felt paralyzed. People probably did think I was a little strange since I allowed those thoughts to keep me planted in the doorway without moving. After what seemed an eternity, I finally moved to find a seat as the thoughts continued to rage. I found a table and proceeded to meet those sitting around it. I could feel my heart beating too fast but I was pretty good at hiding what was going on beneath the surface. I smiled and listened, but didn't say much. I remember feeling very tense, like my shoulders were connected to my ears and I could not relax long enough to drop them and let the tension go. It was not the first time I had experienced this. I had grown accustomed to the heart palpitations, and the tension in my neck and shoulders was barely noticeable anymore. My insecurities had ruled my actions for so long I had learned to live with the effects of them.

As the first speaker came up to give his presentation, I was able to focus long enough to hear another Voice. The thoughts and fears quieted just long enough for me to hear the Lord speak a sentence that would change my life forever. *Anna, people aren't thinking about you.* I imagined God cupping his hands right up to my ear so I was the only one who would hear it. It was the quietest whisper I had ever heard and at first I dismissed it. Then I heard it again; *Anna, child, people aren't thinking about you.*

My thoughts stopped dead as I made the connection. The speaker continued to drone and I remember hearing the click, click of a pen close by. People aren't thinking about me? Surely that is not true. I mean, I have spent so much of my life worrying about what people are thinking of me. I have not been fully present in my life because I've been too busy brooding over what people might think. You are telling me that all this time people have not been thinking of me?

Yes.

My mind exploded with words and I grabbed a pen off the table and took out a blank note pad and started writing. *People aren't thinking about me. Other people aren't worried about me. People don't think about me the way I think they think about me. Why? Because I don't matter? No, because they are too worried about themselves to be thinking about me. In fact, people might actually be wondering what I think of them!*

It was a breakthrough for me. I looked around the table at the people sitting there, chomping on gum, biting their lips, listening to the speaker that I had forgotten all about, and wondered, could it be true? Had I been living under a false belief about what people think? I knew the answer. The answer was *yes,* and from that day on I resolved never to allow that fear to control me again. It was a turning point in my journey of overcoming insecurity, a key to unlock some of the chains that had been holding me hostage. I wrote one more sentence on my pad of paper before the applause of the crowd told me it was time to move on to the next session. *I don't need to hold myself back because of what other people think, because they don't.*

People   don't   think about me the way I think they think

Did you get that? Sometimes I think this is too simple a concept for us to really grasp. Is it really that easy? I believe if we could grasp what kind of power this revelation gives us we would find ourselves in a completely different reality than we are living in now. Remember the pattern common to those suffering from insecurity?

No real sense of identity,

which makes it easy to believe lies,

leading to an unrealistic fear or worry about what other people think.

This new thought was like the bloom of new fruit on a tree. Fragile but true, it began to grow as I tested the validity of the words I heard God speak to my heart. Very slowly, I began to find myself able to walk into a room and be completely myself, confident and sure, because I no longer feared what others thought. I realized the only reason I feared what others thought of me, was because I projected my own negative thoughts, assuming others must think them as well. I saw myself through the lens of my insecurities, and thought everyone else must see me the same way.

The enemy is really good at getting us to think everyone's mind is on us. We are, after all, selfish by nature, so it should not surprise any of us that he would try to get us through our selfishness. It is what makes us think everyone must be saying something about us when we walk into a room, or will blame us when something goes wrong.

In their book *Emotional Intelligence 2.0*, Travis Bradberry and Jean Greaves talk about our ability to effectively manage our behavior and emotions. "Emotional intelligence is your ability to recognize and understand emotions in yourself and others, and your ability to use this awareness to manage your behavior and relationships." They talk about gaining the important skills necessary to mentally take a step back from your emotions and look at them logically before making a decision. It's the satellite perspective we discussed earlier. They say, "You *do* control the thoughts that follow an emotion, and you have a great deal of say in how you react to an emotion—as long as you are aware of it." This is such an important skill to gain when it comes to overcoming our insecurities, especially our fear and worry about what others think of us.

When I worked with students, I texted a lot. But texting does not always work very well, especially if I am busy. I remember having a text message conversation with a student and at some point I was not able to text back for several hours. When I looked at my phone I had several messages from her accusing me of ignoring her, not wanting to talk to her, and disliking her. Had she the emotional skills to mentally take a step back before she sent those messages, she might have realized I might be busy and just could not text back immediately. I understand we're talking about a student who, understandably, is not yet emotionally mature, but the same emotional skill is lacking in many adults as well. We jump to conclusions based on how we feel without first taking a step back and making a logical decision instead of an emotional one.

My husband and I have had the opportunity to minister to young married couples, and I cannot tell you how many stories we hear of arguments between husbands and wives that could have been avoided if we could all learn this important emotional skill. One of the wives I meet with regularly was telling me about an argument they had when her husband came home from work in a bad mood. She immediately jumped to the conclusion that his bad mood was because of something she did or didn't do. She lashed out, without first taking a step back and considering that her husband might have been in a bad mood because of something that happened at work. She didn't mean to start a fight, but her rash, insecure, selfish thinking led to an argument that could have been avoided.

The enemy deviously leads us to believe the lie that life is all about *me,* and thus we become unwitting victims of his plan to sabotage our relationships. Whether the relationship is with a spouse, a child, a friend or acquaintance, when we are self-centered everything anyone says to us is filtered through our insecurity and we can hear things that were never even said. If we had the knowledge and strength to take a step back, remove the lens of our insecurity, and consider someone other than ourselves we could save a lot of time and energy spent on a fight that frays our relational ties. We need to gain the emotional maturity and strength that comes from knowing who we are and assume positive intent in our relationships. The only way to do this is to understand that people don't think about us the way we think they think about us.

When I worked at Life.Church I led a large group of adult volunteer leaders for our youth ministry. I have had the privilege of meeting with several of these leaders to walk with them through certain areas of their lives. Because of my passion for overcoming insecurity, oftentimes we find ourselves talking through some of theirs. One of these leaders confided to me that every time she walks into the leader room all she thinks about is what other people might think of her. She is paralyzed with the fear that someone may not like her. She went on to tell me that if she could just be more like one of the other leaders maybe people would like her. When she told me that, I laughed. What she didn't know was that two weeks before our conversation I had a similar talk with the leader she admired so much. They both struggled with insecurity but neither one of them thought about taking the focus off themselves long enough to realize it.

None of us is exempt from wondering what another person might think of us and no one is exempt from selfish thinking. We all have an underlying desire to be accepted and loved for who we are. The problem comes when we live under an unrealistic fear that we will not be accepted, when we allow this fear to warp our behavior and taint the person we were meant to be. We cannot find our identity in what other people might think of us because people don't think about us the way we think they think about us. I cannot tell you how many times I've held myself back from things I've wanted to do, or altered my behavior because I was afraid of what people might think. If only I had discovered earlier the important skill of taking a step back from my emotions and fears and realized that people were not thinking about me the way I thought they were. In fact, they probably weren't thinking about me at all. And that is a freeing thought!

What if people do think about you?

Let's be honest. For the most part, people don't think about us the way we think they do, because most people are too worried about themselves. However, there are those people who do. I have been observing the behavior of insecurity long enough to realize that there are certain people who will think or speak negatively about another, to our faces or behind our backs. But I have also come to realize usually the reason they do it is because *they* are insecure.

A critical attitude toward another person shows insecurity and jealousy. The primary reason people think negatively or judgmentally about another is from their own insecurity. Remember what our moms used to say when we would get bullied by someone older or bigger than us? "They just say those things to make themselves feel better." Sadly, the same is true in adulthood. You have probably done it yourself; I know I have. It is from our own fear and insecurity that we make critical judgments of others. But now when people make those judgements about us, we need no longer care because we realize this fear of caring what people think is all wrapped up in where we find our identity.

Take a deeper step: In_Security

1. Describe a time you held yourself back or altered your behavior because you feared what others would think of you.

2. What do you think is the root of this fear?

3. What steps can you take to begin to overcome the fear of what others think?

Ten

Identity Theft

When we don't know who we are, we walk through life hoping we are on the right track, constantly feeling we are missing something. When we know who we are and Who we belong to, the path of our life loses some of its mystery and we can know better what to do, and what not to do.

So many of us live our lives trying to please others to find acceptance and validation. What we are really searching for is our identity and the confidence that comes from knowing it, but we are searching for it in the wrong place. We cannot find our validation in the opinion of others because their opinions will change. A people-pleasing mentality pleases no one and keeps us in our self-made prison.

The teenage years are a breeding ground for insecure thoughts and self-doubt. High school alone can leave many teens scarred for life because of emotional decision-making. If students don't have a firm grounding in who they are in Christ, strength from a family identity, or someone speaking positively into their lives, they are liable to fall into any number of traps set by the life-draining system of high school society. Think about it. A new freshman enters high school with no idea of the temptations that await him. He is already going through a crisis of identity with things changing all around him—growing into a newly maturing body, meeting new people, trying not to look dumb and to fit in any way he can without letting anyone find out how intimated he feels. One day after a particularly rough morning of self-doubt and negative self-talk, some of the guys invite him to skip class and go for a smoke. He doesn't necessarily want to do either of these things but he does not want to look stupid or weak, and besides, he feels they are offering something much more, something he has wanted since he entered high school — acceptance. A place to belong. An identity. Sure, it might mean doing something he knows is wrong, but the need for acceptance, is too strong to pass it up. One insecure decision can lead to many other self-destructive decisions as he searches for identity in things that are empty. Before long, he looks up and realizes he is not the person he used to be or wants to be. How did he get here? The problem is, we do not know who we are. If our student had a firm grasp on his identity and knew who he really was, what he stood for, who he belonged to, he might not have fallen into temptation so easily.

The same scenario can be true for anyone who does not have a firm grasp on who they are and the values for which they stand; single ladies, looking for companionship at the expense of their virtue, businessmen or women willing to backslide on integrity to get ahead, even Christ-followers stuck in secret sin when victory is within their grasp. One of the women I meet with shared with me how she falls into this trap. She feels an overwhelming pressure to make sure everyone around her likes her, so in group settings, she finds herself deliberately talking with each person. But friendliness is not her motivation; she is motivated by a fear that if she does not, someone will think badly of her. "I just want people to like me." So I asked her, "What if someone didn't like you? What would that do? What would that change?" She looked at me wide-eyed and confessed, "That would be the worst thing in the world." I asked her why, but she could not come up with a reason. If my friend had a firm grasp on her identity, and liked herself first, she might not feel she has to try so hard to make sure everyone else likes her. It is knowing our true identity that keeps us strong, that helps us know how to live our lives. When you know who you are, you will know what to do.

A friend told me recently how much she hates her job. Her real dream was to cook, to go to culinary school and maybe open a restaurant. When I asked her why she didn't go for it, she explained that her uncle had offered to pay for her schooling if she got a degree in accounting. "You know, something realistic, and safe," she explained with disgust, quoting her uncle. "I didn't want to disappoint him, I mean he was offering to pay for school! So I agreed, but now I totally regret it." How sad. This girl gave up her dream because she didn't want to disappoint someone. I understand having school paid for is a huge enticement, but I wonder what her life might look like if she had chased her own dream without worrying about what others might think. If she had known who she was and had a strong resolve about what she wanted from life, might her decision have been different? She allowed fear to hold her back, and now she hates the life she leads.

No one knows this way of living better than I. Before I realized where I could find true validation, my true identity, I was trying to find my fulfillment in what other people thought. I was basing my sense of worth on the perceived opinions of other human beings who might be just as insecure as I. If someone liked me I was on top of the world. If someone said something negative, disliked me for any reason, or just didn't show me attention, my mood would plummet and no one could talk me out of my self-focused, self-deprecating thoughts. I had no anchor to hold on to, no stabilizer to keep me from reacting to the way other people viewed me, and because of that I had no idea who I was. I had no emotional stability to keep me from subjecting myself to anyone who might give me even a little acceptance or validation and no knowledge to help me overcome a fear that held me hostage for so long. But through the pain I experienced along my journey, I realized I could not live my life for the approval of others any longer. It just wasn't working for me. God used my past hurt to break me. He was the only One who could heal the broken places of my heart. He showed me that the true source of strength and acceptance comes only from Him. I know one reason He allowed me to experience that pain is so I could share it with others. God drew me to Himself and in Him I found my true identity. I can tell you honestly that when I did, I stopped living my life for other people. Their opinions of me no longer matter, because I have found true validation that can never be taken away from me. Now I live for Him and Him alone. Could God possibly be using your past pain to draw you close to Him? Might He want to show you the true source of your identity?

I confess that one of the reasons I have put off writing this book and sharing my story is because of the fear of what others would think. I don't want to look like a failure. Early in my writing career I sent several things off for publication. I was accepted maybe two or three times, but mostly rejected. Each rejection was like another layer of hurt on my already wounded heart, confirming once again the lie that I had nothing to offer. I quit writing for several years because I feared further rejection. Fearing what others might think kept me in a state of direct disobedience to God. Do you have any idea what it feels like to live in direct disobedience to God? It's awful! You lose intimacy with Him when you are not doing what you know He has called you to do. Every time I would spend time with Him praying for a new word, His simple, continuous, loving response spoke to my heart, "You haven't yet done what I asked. It hasn't changed and it won't until you obey." When I realized I had no excuse to put it off anymore I started seriously writing. My identity is not found in whether people read it or not. My identity is found in who I am to Him and living from the strength my obedience to Him gives me. Realizing this gave me a power I did not have before.

Our identity is not found in our accomplishments or failures. It is not found in the people we spend our time with, or even in the thoughts we have of ourselves. It is found in Him. The unchanging, all powerful, creator of our souls. God continues to reveal this to me. He reminds me that He already knows everything about me and He still loves me. He knows my secret sins, fears, worries, and thoughts and He still accepts me for who I am. The very thing I had been searching for in others, I could find in Him, and *He* never changes so my identity is rock solid, as long as I stay connected to Him.

Do You Want to be Free?

I know some of you must be thinking, "Great! All I have to do to overcome my insecurity is find my identity in Christ. Like I haven't heard that before." I understand the frustration. I have read countless books that told me the same thing, but I still found myself in the same place as before. I don't just want to *tell* you what you have to do to overcome your insecurities. I want to *show* you how to do it.

In the next few chapters we will uncover the secret of overcoming our insecurities. We will discover how to find our identity in Christ and keep it there. We will understand how to overcome the lies that keep us bound. I want to give you tools to help you truly find freedom, but first you have to want it. I mean really want it, with everything in you. You have to have a passion for it that will propel you forward when the tough times come. You have to resolve to be intentional every day until you learn to walk in freedom.

I was reading in the Gospel of John the other day the story about Jesus encountering a man who had been paralyzed for thirty-eight years! This man lay by a pool that many thought had the power to heal. He was never able to get into the pool when the water was stirred so there he sat. Jesus asked him a question that caught me off guard, "Do you want to get well?" Of course this man wanted to get well! He had been paralyzed for most of his life. Why would Jesus ask such a question? Jesus was not just asking if he wanted to get well, he was asking how badly this paralyzed man wanted to get well. After thirty-eight years this was the only life he had ever known. Was he afraid of change? Was he secretly afraid to get well because he was afraid of what he might have to do next — find a job, live a life without the constant handouts of others? Had he found comfort in his current situation because that was all he ever knew? What about us? Have we found a false sense of security in our insecurity? Are we afraid to be free because it would mean things would have to change? Don't allow the fear of change to sabotage your freedom. (See appendix B "Self Sabotage" in the back of the book.)

So, do you want to be free? How badly do you want it? The tools and insights I am sharing in this fight to overcome insecurity will never be enough unless we match them with an unrelenting desire to be free. How many times have we heard other people complain, saying how much they wish they could lose twenty pounds, or learn to play the piano, or have a better job or improve something in their lives? If we want something badly enough there should be nothing that can stand in the way of getting it. True desire for God's best for us is the only thing that will keep us going when it feels like we have nothing left. Do you want to be free from your insecurities? Christ within you is the power that brings you freedom. How much do you want it?

It's time to put ideas into practice.

Take a deeper step: In_Security

1. List some of the areas other than Christ in which you have tried to find your validation, self-worth or identity.

2. In what ways have those areas fallen short in showing you your true identity?

3. What areas of self-sabotage have you struggled with most? What is your next step in overcoming the habit of self-sabotage? (Appendix B)

Part 3

Promise

Pursuit

Prize

Eleven

Freedom

Freedom. We long for it. Something deep inside of us tells us we were made for it. We honor the great men and women who have fought to defend it. Many people around the world would do anything to get it. Freedom is the reason great movies like *Braveheart* give us chills when we see a man give his life for it. We know we are meant to live in freedom, but sadly, so many of us don't. Yes, we may live in a free country, have freedom of speech, freedom of religion, freedom to make our own decisions, but deep down in our heart many of us are still living in bondage.

I know what it is like to live in bondage, to face each day living at half capacity. I know what it feels like to be so afraid of breaking free that I almost found comfort in the chains that kept me bound. But now I know what it feels like to have those chains fall away and the burden I was carrying to lift off my shoulders. There is a lightness about my spirit that I didn't have before, a freedom that keeps me actively living in the present instead of fading away, brooding on my own negative thoughts. I know bondage and I know freedom. Freedom is better, by far.

I can honestly tell you that I believe God has revealed to me the secret of overcoming insecurity, because it happened in my own life. I feel as if I have lived two different lives, been two different people. The Anna imprisoned by fear, worry, self-doubt and uncertainty is the antithesis of who I am now. Do I still have moments of worry, self-doubt and uncertainty? Yes, but I no longer live in that prison. I have found the key and my prayer is that through this knowledge you will find that same freedom for your own life.

The Truth will Set You Free

The key that unlocks those chains, the secret to overcoming insecurity, the power we have been given to fight off the lies is truth. If believing lies keeps us in the bondage of insecurity than certainly believing truth is the key that sets us free. God says it very clearly in John 8:32 "Then you will know the truth and the truth will set you free." Truth is the gift God has given us to set us free from chains that keep us bound. If we do not know the truth, we do not know freedom. If each step we take is not firmly grounded in the truth of God, we are walking a tightrope over the chasm of death and destruction. Sadly, that is just what the enemy wants.

But what is truth, and how do we use it to unlock the prison of insecurity? In His three years of ministry Jesus called Himself many things. "I am the resurrection and the life..." John 11:25. "I am the Gate..." John 10:9. "I am the Vine..." John 15:5. But no synonym for the name of Jesus is more powerful than, "I am the Way, the Truth and the Life; no one comes to the Father but through Me." John 14:6.

Jesus is the Truth, and a relationship with Him is the only way we will ever know true freedom. Without Him we are nothing. He is the Author and Perfecter of our faith and the only Person who will ever satisfy our loved-starved, significance-searching hearts. Trying to live a life of freedom without being connected to His boundless grace is a counterfeit life, nothing like the life God had in mind for us when we were created. If we want to live the abundant, free life God designed, we must start with Jesus.

You may already have a relationship with Jesus. Perhaps you've been following Him for quite some time, you go to church, occasionally read the Word, serve others and live a generally good life. Yet, many people with a relationship with Jesus are still struggling to break free from the hurts and hang-ups in their life. Having a relationship with Jesus is simply where we start. To continue growing we must use the resources He's given us as weapons in this battle for freedom. The number one resource He has given us is the Word of God. There's a reason it is called the Sword of the Spirit (Ephesians 6:17). It is there for us to pick up and do battle against the lies of the enemy. Knowing and applying his Word to your life is the work of freedom. Sadly, many Christ-followers either aren't in the Word on a regular basis, or if they are, simply check it off as another to-do. They don't realize that His Word is the Ring of Keys which unlock the ancient, iron-walled doors of insecurity. But that is exactly what the Word can be in our lives. Your enemy knows this and will do anything he can to keep you from picking up the Word because he sees it for what it is: A weapon that cuts to the quick of his deception, a key that frees his captives, and a standard to which everything should be compared.

It reminds me of the analogy of how federal agents are trained to spot counterfeit money. Perhaps you've heard this before. To identify counterfeit money, agents don't study the counterfeit. They study real money. They commit to memory the look, feel, and smell of real money first, so that when they come across a counterfeit they will know. Training in identifying the counterfeit starts with studying the genuine. We could say it like this: training in identifying the enemy's lies starts with studying God's Truth. If God's Word is living in us, and we've committed to memory what He says about us, we will be able to recognize when something comes to us that does not line up with the Truth. We will spot the counterfeit because we know the Real Thing.

Similarly, employers who want to reduce loss of income for their businesses will train their employees on how to spot a counterfeit bill. They are also trained on what real money looks and feels like, but they are also encouraged to hold a bill up to the light to help them identify it as the real thing. They are looking for a magnetic strip, a watermark, and other identifying aspects of a genuine bill that can only be seen when it is held up to the light. How true is this for us as we talk about finding freedom from lies. The enemy works in darkness and it is in an atmosphere of darkness where sin and deception do their best growth. Your enemy's hope is that you will keep your insecurities in darkness. He doesn't want you to talk about them, think about them, or share them with others. Why do you think he tries so hard to make you feel insecure about yourself? So you'll keep your mouth shut and continue on like nothing needs to change. But that is a counterfeit life in desperate need of the shining light of Jesus to reveal the dark dungeons in which we are hiding. God's Word is that shining light.

Bring it to the Light

When I was struggling to overcome my insecurities God led

me to write down the top three lies I believed about myself—
the enemy's deception, out of my head, into the light, and star-
ing at me on paper. I'm suggesting you also take some time to
think about the top three lies you believe about yourself. There
is room at the end of this chapter to write them down. Think
about your inner self-talk over the past two weeks, the
thoughts that go through your head when you are in an un-
comfortable situation, or when you want to start something
new and unknown. Do you recall the last time you felt insecure
or uncertain about yourself or a situation? What lies have you
believed without realizing it? Is there pain from your past you
are carrying that needs to be laid down for good?

I understand this may be a painful exercise. I recommend doing this with a trusted friend or mentor if it seems overwhelming. Take a break from reading if you have to, go do something
so you can think, but then come back and write those insecurities down.

As I shared earlier, the top three lies I believed about myself
when I was stuck in the bondage of my own insecurity were:

1. I'm fat—therefore I'm not a whole person, and have
    nothing to offer.

2. I'm ugly because I'm fat.

3. No one wants to be around me because of the way I look. I'm a reject.

You may write something like:

I'm single and I'll never find someone who will love me.

I'm not pretty.

I'll never amount to anything.

I'm damaged.

No one could ever love me.

I'm not good enough.

I'm a failure.

No one sees me.

I'm not living up to my expectations.

You know what plagues you, now write it down. There's something about getting these lies on paper that makes them lose some of their strength. You will begin to realize how the enemy has tricked you into believing something that really has no power — because it's not true. The only power it has is the power your belief has been giving it. It's time to move your belief to the real thing.

Using Truth to Counter Lies

Now it is time to open that Bible. Searching for truths to counter your lies may take a few days, or months, maybe even years, but it is worth the investment of a lifetime. If God's Word is truth, and truth is the key that sets us free, we must know what His Word says about us if we want to win the battle of insecurity. Do you know His Word?

Using God's Word, find scriptures that counter each of the lies you wrote down. Think of each of these scriptures as a separate key that will unlock the chains of your lies.

When I was searching for my keys, I read through several scriptures until I found ones that spoke directly to my heart. If you're not familiar with the Bible or struggle to understand it, a good place to start is in Psalms. This book in the middle of your Bible is full of astounding truths that have the power to disintegrate the strongholds in your life. Search for them. When you read something that strikes a chord in your spirit, write it down. When you read a truth that leaves you with chills, it might just be the one for you to take as your own. Memorize it. Here are just some of the keys that set me free from my lies.

I'm fat, therefore I'm ugly and have nothing to offer— "The King is enthralled with your beauty, honor Him for He is your Lord!" Psalm 45:11.

No one likes me because of the way I look. No one wants to be around me. I'm a reject— "I have chosen you to be my special treasure." Deuteronomy 7:6.

These truths spoke to my heart in a way I can't explain. I'm beautiful and I'm chosen. The two things I desired most in life I found in His Word. I wrote them down and began to memorize them. Any time a lie would hit, I would have a truth ready to do battle. It was hard at first. It wasn't something that happened overnight. There were times that I still allowed my insecurities to hold me back. Sometimes it felt like I would take one step forward, and two steps back. But I trudged forward, knowing I had to change my thinking. Any time I began to notice those old feelings of fear and insecurity I would mentally take a step back and say to myself, "No, I'm not going to believe those lies anymore. I'm beautiful and I'm chosen because He says so." Sometimes I would speak the verse quietly to remind myself of who God says I am. It took practice to change my thinking. As with anything we want to become better at, we must practice.

After several months of determined effort, with God's help, I rewired my brain and believing truth became more natural to me than believing lies. I understood that the same power I had given the lies in my life, I could now give to truth. It was my choice all along. I saw that if I believed a truth long enough and hard enough, soon it would become my reality. I had the power to change my thinking and my reality and you have that same power. If you believe what God says about you, find your identity in Him, and step into opportunities He leads you to, you will act out of that perception, which is the truth, and it will become your reality —your new life.

As I began to walk in the confidence of His truth, the lies slowly fell away. When they did, my physical weight seemed to fall away with them. When people hear I have lost a significant amount of weight, they always ask how I did it. I tell them it happened from the inside out. I lost more than the pounds, I lost my bondage. I became free on the inside, and the outside shell followed. I wanted to mirror the girl I was becoming on the inside with the girl everyone saw on the outside. I wanted people to have a reason to ask so I could share with them the amazing knowledge God revealed to me. His truth changed me, truly changed me, from the inside out, and His truth can do the same for anyone who will believe it.

My friend Dea, for example, struggled with many lies she started believing when she went through an ugly divorce. She replayed the ruthless words her husband told her, over and over in her mind like a broken record. She believed she was never good enough, and so would always overcompensate by trying to make everyone around her happy. She was a self-professed people-pleaser. However, she knew she was drowning in the sea of her insecurities and needed help.

I'll never forget the day I met Dea. She approached me during one of our staff gatherings, and said some of the most encouraging words. She said she had been watching me as I interacted with others, that she saw a sense of security in me, a sense of freedom that she wanted for herself and she wondered if maybe we could have coffee sometime soon. I was honored and surprised. Dea is in her sixties and she was asking a twenty-something girl to help her overcome her insecurities. I was overjoyed, not only because through this I gained a very valuable friendship, but also because God showed me once more that He wanted to use my journey to help others find freedom.

We began to meet once a week to talk about the lies she had accepted. She knew the scriptures better than I did, but never saw them as absolute answers that could change the negative thoughts that bound her. As she allowed God's truth to invade the painful areas of her life, she gained more freedom. Over the next few months I watched this beautiful woman transform from the inside out into a new creation. She dropped about thirty pounds, started dressing in a way that told everyone she respected herself, and had a confidence that could only be explained by the Truth of God's Word. I came to call her Sassy D. Now when she walks into a room she lights it up, instead of fading into the background as she did before. She has found freedom in God's truth and everyone can tell something has changed. She no longer lives under the lie that she isn't good enough. She found the truths that countered the lies and unlocked the chains for good. Since that time she went back to school and graduated Summa Cum Laude in Distinction and has opened a firm where she counsels individuals to understand their significance and use their passion to live a life of influential leadership. The Dea I sat across from over coffee at our very first meeting could not have done all that. It was the power of freedom at work in her life.

That same power is there for you in God's Word. All it takes is a willing heart to search it out and apply it to your own situation. What could you accomplish if you were free? Who's lives might be forever changed if you were released from what holds you back? What genius idea, creative resource, or life-giving word could be shared if you weren't locked in the devil's deception?

Let's look at the lies I wrote above and the truths that will unravel them.

I'm single and I'll never find someone who will love me. —

"Delight yourself in the Lord and He will give you the desires of your heart." Psalm 37:4

I'm not pretty. — "I praise you because I am fearfully and wonderfully made." Psalm 139:14

I'll never amount to anything. — "'For I know the plans I have for you', declares the Lord, 'plans to prosper you and not to harm you, plans to give you hope and a future.'" Jeremiah 29:11

I'm damaged. — "He who was seated on the throne said, 'I am making everything new!'" Revelation 21:5

No one could ever love me. — "I have loved you with an everlasting love; I have drawn you with unfailing kindness." Jeremiah 31:3

I'm not good enough. — "For we are God's handiwork, created in Christ Jesus to do good works, which God prepared in advance for us to do." Ephesians 2:10

I'm a failure. — "No, in all these things we are more than conquerors through him who loved us." Romans 8:37

No one sees me. —"The Lord himself watches over you! The Lord stands beside you as your protective shade." Psalm 121:5NLT

Truth: You are God's workmanship, created in Christ Jesus to do good works. Truth: You are God's masterpiece, perfectly woven together and known before birth! Truth: You are God's chosen one, set apart as His child before you ever took a breath! That is the truth, no matter how you feel, what you think, or what others say. There's no way to get around it. Truth is truth no matter who believes it. Why not believe it? When you find a scripture you believe is the one God designed especially for your liberation, I encourage you to memorize it, study it, pick it apart. There may be even more He wants to reveal to you behind the meanings of certain words, translations and phrases. Make it yours. Own it. Live it.

When we apply God's truths to our lives, the old lies will lose their power. It is through the consistent practice of seeking out, believing, and speaking truth to ourselves that we will find the freedom for which we are searching. It cannot be done just once or twice a month, we must adopt it as a lifestyle. The rewards will absolutely change your life, I promise.

Take a deeper step: In_Security

1. Write down the top three lies you believe about yourself.

2. What are the root of these lies? Can you think back to where they may have originated?

3. What truths have you found that will counter those lies? (This may take some time, come back to this section as you continue to study, but DO NOT neglect this step.)

Twelve

Fitting the Pieces Together

My family and I love to work puzzles. During the winter months and around the holidays you can bet there is an unfinished puzzle sitting out somewhere, waiting to be completed. There is something therapeutic about putting together a puzzle, that jumble of pieces that you know fit together to make a beautiful picture. You might even have a sample of that picture on the outside of the box— an example of what you are working on to help you stay on track. It can be fun and challenging, especially when you are doing it with other people. Fun, because it gives you that jolt of accomplishment when you fit piece after piece together, challenging, because even though you know all the pieces fit together, for a while you cannot seem to make heads or tails of what it is you are working on. And then, just when you want to give up, you find a fit that keeps you hopeful that you really can complete it. Puzzles are funny things really. We spend all this time working them, fitting the pieces together, trying to finish, while all we are going to do when we are done is crumple it up and put the pieces back in the box. We think the finished outcome is our goal, but the truth is, it is the process where we found the most enjoyment. The minute we finish a puzzle, we pull out another to start it over again.

Finding freedom from insecurity is very similar. It's not exactly a destination or an end goal we are trying to achieve, it is a continual process, a journey, of taking our thoughts captive and making them obedient to Christ, a journey of a life reliant on Him. Once you overcome one insecurity, there will be another to overcome. It's one way we can be sure we are constantly growing and changing. We will always be in need of God's continual power and guidance to walk in freedom. He created us that way, with a deep longing satisfied only by Him. It is an everyday decision to put the pieces of God's truth together in our minds to discover our true identity. We even have a preview picture in His Word, which we must look at often, to keep us on track. It is in the journey to freedom that we find the greatest peace, because it is there that we are most reliant on Him.

Freedom Envy

When you do find that freedom you will know it, you will feel it. You won't have to wonder if you're free—you won't have to ask someone to make sure. But do not be surprised if you run into a few naysayers on this journey—people who are not yet free themselves. They may be jealous of your freedom and do not know how to handle the growing, changing, and freed you. Do not take it personally. They are fighting their own battles and need your love, grace, and acceptance to start their own journey toward freedom.

Some of my relationships were affected by my new-found freedom, mainly friends I spent time with because we had negativity in common. When I no longer put others down to make myself feel better, our ties became frayed. When I no longer participated in insecure, negative self-talk, we didn't have a lot to say. As I grew in my freedom, they accused me of thinking I was better than they. They said they felt judged by me because I started standing for truth instead of gossip, encouragement instead of slander. They did not know how to relate to me anymore, nor I to them.

I had breakfast with a woman last week who was experiencing some of the same dilemma. She is allowing God to reveal to her the lies she believed about herself, and accepting His truth instead. She no longer lives under the shadow of bondage. She is captivating, encouraging, and full of the love of God. But there was something troubling her. Since embracing her new-found freedom, the other women in her life have treated her very differently. Cut-downs, negativity, hurtful words, and hateful attitudes. She asked me, "What did I do to get this kind of response?" Nothing, except get free. As women, if we are not careful, we can struggle with petty jealousy. I call it Freedom Envy, caused by not being content in ourselves. We see another woman walking in the freedom we wish we had and something rises up in us. Discontentment, depression, obsession, anger, jealousy, hatred, they take control of our attitudes and we lash out causing our insecurity to pull us even tighter into bondage.

I used to struggle with this very thing. Here's a little vulnerability for you. A girl I grew up with seemed to have everything together. She was beautiful, always encouraging others, full of life, and popular with everyone. I found myself thinking that if I was like her then maybe I would not hate who I was so much. I tried to emulate her. I watched how she dressed, talked, and interacted with others. I tried to learn her habits or what it was she did to be so well-liked and confident. Through my little bout of obsession with this girl's life I saw one thing that stood out as a constant. Jesus. It was evident her source of strength and hope came from something much bigger than herself and the good news was that I could have it too. Through that time, I realized the truth that I would not make a very good, her, but I make an excellent me. No one else could be me.

Through this, and many other realizations of truth along my

journey I found my true identity and rested in the security it brought. Not long after I started walking in freedom I got a call from a girl confessing her jealousy of me. She told me, "I find myself thinking that if I could just be like Anna, then I would like myself. Then, maybe people would want to be around me." I was able to tell her the same thing God revealed to me: "You wouldn't make a very good Anna, but you make an excellent you!"

See, it's not the person we envy, it's the freedom they have found. People who are comfortable in their own skin draw others to themselves. At rest with who they are, they allow others to be at rest in who they are. They do not compete, compare, or control. When people are free, it shows. When they are no longer bound by insecurities and lies, they are able to be fully present, care-free and happier. That's what we all want, isn't it, not to be someone else, but to be the person God created, unhindered by the doubt, fear and insecurity that holds us back?

None of us knows what someone else might have to go through to overcome their insecurities. No one but the seeker can appreciate the pain, tears, doubts, fears and questions that go into finding one's identity in Christ. It takes work, dedication, faith, and the encouragement of others. So please, let's not allow our own insecurities to steal another's joy and freedom. This Christian walk is truly a fight. We are all in battle with our common enemy; let's not be in battle with one another. We need to place ourselves among others who will encourage us toward freedom, not hold us back by freedom envy. Let's become freedom fighters—in our own lives—and in the lives of others and surround ourselves with those who can also be freedom fighters for us. After all, we will never make a very good someone else, but we each make an excellent "me".

Leaky

Have you ever noticed, as humans we are incredibly forgetful? I call it leaky. We can read a life-changing book, listen to an inspiring video, or have a great conversation that starts to make a change in our lives, but not two weeks later, oftentimes, we are right back in the same place we started. I have met with a number of women who admit that once they have reached freedom from their insecurities they think they have arrived. They stop doing the things they did to get out of the pit of insecurity, thinking that the freedom they have found will carry them. Their confidence begins to soar and they ride the wave until they look up and realize they've drifted too far from the safety of the shore. The sad truth is, we are leaky. We forget the words that set us free, the truths that made us whole, and we slip, ever so slowly, back into our old habits and our old way of thinking. We begin to neglect time in God's Word and forget how His presence was the key that set us free. It is a human problem. We forget. We get lazy. We leak. It reminds me of the scripture in Revelation 2:5 that says, "Consider how far you have fallen. Repent and do the things you did at first."

I have said it before, but it bears repeating. Overcoming insecurity is not just a destination. It is a daily journey of taking our thoughts captive and making them obedient to Christ. Like any other sin, addiction, or struggle we want to overcome, we must continually pursue a life-style away from insecurity. This means different things for different people, but here are some things you can do when you feel yourself slipping back into those old habits of bondage.

Check your time with God. When we start to feel great about ourselves and the way things are going, sometimes our relationship with God fades into the background. We need to make sure time with the Lord is our highest priority. When things are good, rejoice and praise Him with thanksgiving. When things are hard, pour out your heart to Him and immerse yourself in His truth. The enemy is just waiting for you to let your guard down. Don't let him catch you unaware.

Make others the focus. Remember, insecurity is a selfish sin. Continue to overcome it by focusing your thoughts and attention on others. When you start to feel the pull of an insecure, self-seeking attitude, think of someone you could encourage. Send a message, text, or make a phone call to someone who might just need a listening ear, or an encouraging word. You will be amazed how much encouraging someone else can actually encourage you as well. "A generous person will prosper; whoever refreshes others will be refreshed." Proverbs 11:25.

Don't dwell on the negative. Insecurity is fueled by negative thinking. When you catch yourself spending too much time in the murky waters of negativity it is time to give yourself a mental shake. Sometimes I feel my old habit of comparison trying to work its way into my thoughts and I have to say out loud, "No, no, no, no, no, I am not going there." I did it just today! I felt threatened by something I saw on social media and I started to compare myself. Instead, I praised the person's accomplishments and the sin of comparison lost its control. Positive thinking, positive action, is the antidote.

Truth trumps all. Are you dwelling on the truth, or are you listening to lies? If the lies are starting to take over again it's time to get those scriptures out. Do what you did before. Don't get this far in your journey and forget what got you here in the first place. It can be so easy to slowly fall back into your old habits, but remember, it wasn't your strength that got you where you are now, so don't rely on your strength to keep you from slipping. It was, and always will be, in the strength of Christ and His Truth that we find our freedom. James 1:22-25 states clearly, "Do not merely listen to the word, and so deceive yourselves. Do what it says. Anyone who listens to the word but does not do what it says is like someone who looks at his face in a mirror and, after looking at himself, goes away and immediately forgets what he looks like. But whoever looks intently into the perfect law *that gives freedom*, and continues in it—not forgetting what they have heard, but doing it—they will be blessed in what they do." (Emphasis mine.)

So, we have learned that people do not think about us the way we think they do and we have learned that God's truths are the keys that set us free. Those two things should be enough to free us from the chains that bind us. But I realize those pieces alone may not be everything you need. I grew up knowing and memorizing scripture, but still found myself in a prison. What if you know God's Word but have trouble believing it for yourself? You can know how to get free and still be in bondage. It takes more than knowledge to be free. It takes action. In the last chapter we will uncover what that missing piece may be, and find ourselves identifying with this thought from the apostle Paul: "I press on toward the goal to win the prize for which God has called me heavenward in Christ Jesus." (Philippians 3:14).

Take a deeper step: In_Security

1. Have you ever struggled with "freedom envy"? What were the circumstances and how did/do you handle feeling that way?

2. How do the thoughts we've discussed in the previous chapters help you in your journey to overcome your insecurities?

3. If you never had another insecure thought again what would your life look like? How would it be different from the life you're living now? What keeps you from that life?

Thirteen

"The prize of freedom is love. The prize of love is freedom."—Anna Light

This quote from Dale Carnegie couldn't be more true. "Inaction breeds doubt and fear. Action breeds confidence and courage." We could say it like this: If you want to stay insecure, do nothing. If you want freedom, do something! Action is what will get you from dreaming of freedom to walking in freedom. It is not until you take an action step of faith that you can begin your journey to freedom. James says it pretty clearly too. "In the same way, faith by itself, if it is not accompanied by action is dead.... As the body without the spirit is dead, so faith without deeds is dead." James 2:17,18 & 26.

Let's say you have found some scriptures to help you fight the lies that have taken root in your mind. Do you believe those scriptures? Do you believe those scriptures are true for *you*? God's truths are transforming only to the extent they are believed, received and absorbed. Just as a healthy meal cannot bring nourishment unless it is eaten and digested, God's Word must be eaten and digested to make it a living part of us. We must learn how to make His truths our own. If you only ever read about how to do a pull-up, you'll never gain the strength to actually do one. Practice is what makes our muscles grow, and it is in the daily practice of actively believing God's Word that true transformation will be found.

When I was struggling to get free I would read certain scriptures and think, "Well, this may be true for other people, but it is not true for me. I'm not special enough; not good enough." The words stayed flat and empty because I was not actively believing them for myself. My insecurities exempted me from the power of God's Word. But I soon realized how incredibly damaging that line of thinking was in my life. I'm no different from anyone else. If scripture can apply to others' lives, it can apply to mine as well. By thinking that, I put myself on a pedestal thinking I needed another set of scriptures—a stronger set—to help me overcome my lies. But I didn't. And neither do you. We just need to actively believe that the truth set in the scriptures is for us.

How do you actively believe something? Essentially you have to have proof, or you have to have trust. Knowing if someone can be trusted depends greatly on how well you know that person. If, for example, you had a flat tire and someone offered you a ride, your response to the offer would depend on how well you knew the person. If the offer came from a total stranger, you would probably decline; you know nothing of his character, and were probably taught at a young age not to trust strangers. If it came from an acquaintance, you might accept; you have no reason to feel you can't trust this person, but maybe you don't want to be a burden to them, after all, you only know them so well. But if a family member or close friend were to stop, you would accept without a moment's hesitation; you know this person well, you feel safe in their presence, and trust him (or her) completely to have your best interests at heart.

The same is true when it comes to actively believing the truth of scripture. Your ability to believe that what God's Word says about you is true, is directly related to how much you trust Him, and how much you trust Him, is directly related to how well you know Him. If God is a stranger to you, you will have no reason to trust Him, His Word or His character, and likely won't. If you have only a casual acquaintance with Him, you may want to believe Him, but don't really know Him well enough to be sure you can trust Him. You don't want to be a burden, and worry Him with little ol' you, and so you may struggle with accepting His Word for yourself, or going to Him at all. If, however, you are as close to Him as a best friend, or as intimate as a lover, then you know you can trust Him and the truth of His Word; you feel safe in his presence, you have built a deep relationship through time and circumstances that have proven His love and faithfulness to you. You know He cares about every aspect of your life, even the small things. When you read His Word you know the scriptures were written just for you because your heart has been captivated by his love.

Trust and Love

Coming out of the bondage of insecurity likely means that we find it difficult to trust others, even God Himself. This is where I found myself. I was on the cusp of realizing true freedom and yet my lack of trust was holding me back. Could the words I found in the Bible really set me free? I knew the only way to really believe God's Word for myself was simply to get to know God better. I had to know He was trustworthy. I had to discover it for myself, not because someone else told me. I had to make it my own, and put my faith into action.

For months, I spent numerous nights studying God's Word, writing my thoughts, memorizing scripture. During that time God revealed to me, through various stories in His Word, that

He really is worthy of my trust and He really does what He says He's going to do.

I realized this while reading through the gospels, the first four books in the new testament. Throughout each gospel, Jesus talked about his death, prophesying what would inevitably happen to Him to fulfill the scriptures. His disciples had a hard time believing it. Maybe they didn't want to believe it. In their minds Jesus would become King, but they had their own ideas of what that would look like. I wonder how many times things happen it our lives that look much different from the way we imagine? Peter especially had a hard time believing Jesus and even rebuked him at one point. I wonder how many times our own doubt makes us rebuke the words of God in our lives because we are unwilling to believe them for ourselves. When we fear being found out for who we really are, do we, like Peter, deny the Truth instead of surrendering to it?

The beautiful thing I realized about Peter is what happened after he realized Jesus was a Man of His word. After Peter denied Jesus and after Jesus forgave him, something changed in Peter that made him different from that moment forward. For three years he walked with Him and learned from Him, but I like to imagine it was that moment while Peter watched his King ascend into heaven, he was finally able to say, "You were right all along. You knew what you were doing this whole time." It's only with that kind of unwavering trust that Peter, along with the other disciples, could have endured all they went through to spread the gospel of Jesus Christ. And it is that kind of trust that you and I need to be transformed by His truth. It's the kind of trust that removes all traces of doubt and fear. It's the kind of trust that brings freedom.

It wasn't just trust that propelled the disciples into their God-given calling with courage and passion. It was also love. During my journey to freedom through the truth of God's Word, I found that love. It was inevitable. I fell in love with Christ and His astonishing grace that accepted me for who I was. His scriptures became my scriptures. His truths became my truths. I could trust Him at His Word because I fell in love with my Creator. I guess you could say that in those few months I "found my identity in Christ," which simply means I became free— from bondage, from lies, from my own self-degrading thoughts, and the worry of what other people thought. I knew who I was and I did not care if anyone else knew who I was. God knew and that became enough.

There was a certain confidence that came with this revelation. Love will do that to a person. Have you ever noticed someone newly in love? They walk on clouds and nothing can bring them down. That is how I felt. No longer did I walk into a room and cower, wondering who was paying attention to me. No longer did I hold myself back, afraid of what people might think. No longer did I hear the self-loathing lies of the enemy anytime I had a quiet moment. I had searched for God's truth, found it, believed it, absorbed it, and it unlocked my cage. I felt like I could finally fly. The girl I knew on the inside started coming out. I started losing weight with so much more ease. I didn't do it because I knew I needed to. I did it because I wanted to. I did it because I knew taking care of my body was one way I could honor God. It wasn't some kind of discipline I was forcing on myself, it was a desire that came from within that kept me motivated. It was love because I was spending time with Love Himself. Love for Christ, because I knew him better than I ever had, and finally love for myself.

Love Thy Neighbor as Thyself

During my journey to freedom I had to face the fact that one of my greatest obstacles was that I did not love myself. There were days I hated myself. I put myself down in my head and out loud. Looking back now, I realize it was the enemy working against me, but during my times with Jesus I really uncovered a missing piece of the puzzle—learning to love myself.

I read Donald Miller's *Blue Like Jazz* during this season and the chapter on Love really uncovered something I had never thought of before. Mark 12:31 says, "Love the Lord your God with all your heart and with all your soul and with all your mind and with all your strength, ... and love your neighbor as you love yourself. There is no commandment greater than these." Miller comments, *"[God] was telling me I would never talk to my neighbor the way I talked to myself, and that somehow I had come to believe it was wrong to kick other people around but it was okay to do it to myself. It was as if God had put me in a plane and flown me over myself so I could see how I was connected, all the neighborhoods that were falling apart because I would not let myself receive love from myself, from others, or from God. And I wouldn't receive love because it felt so wrong. It didn't feel humble, and I knew I was supposed to be humble."*

There is a big difference between being humble and not loving yourself. Being humble doesn't mean you are always down on yourself or think less of yourself. It simply means you think of yourself less. It means you know your place and you know God's place. If God loves you, you are worth loving. Read that again. If God loves you, you are worth loving. I had to come to the painful realization that even though I might not like myself or my current circumstances, I needed to learn how to love myself. How could I love my neighbor as myself, if I didn't even love myself? Could I truly love my family, friends, husband or children if I could not receive love for myself? Only when I learned to love myself could I accept God's love and His Truth for me as my own. The same is true of you.

When I lived on my own, I had a friend who had the hardest time receiving love. I learned she had been molested as a teenager and carried such a burden of guilt, pain and confusion because of something someone else did to her. She couldn't understand unconditional love. She didn't understand why I chose to love her. She thought she needed to do something to earn my friendship, earn my love, but I kept telling her, "I don't love you because of what you can do for me. I just love you, for you." She continued to give in to the lies and started treating me unfairly. She pushed me away and did things to hurt me, but I knew she only pushed me away because she was afraid. One afternoon I got a call that she had taken a bottle of pills because she just couldn't take living like she was any longer. I rushed to her apartment and we sat on the bed and cried. I told her she would not understand unconditional love until she learned to love herself. And she could never love herself until she surrendered to God's love. I could tell that hit a chord with her. She admitted she had never loved herself but she had just found her worth in the love she received from others. She pushed me away to see what I would do and when I continued to show her love, she did not have control of the situation any longer. I did not love her from my own strength because, believe me, there were days I did not want to love her. I loved her because of Christ's love. I loved her because I had learned to love myself. When we learn to love ourselves because Christ loves us, giving unconditional love to others comes a lot easier, because when we live in the security of Jesus' love it enables us to need less, and love others more.

Maybe you are like my friend and you find yourself struggling to accept God's love because you don't love yourself. Any number of things that happened in our past can cause us to sink into this pit. I encourage you, if you're struggling to find the ability to love yourself, seek help from a mentor or counselor. That may be the first step on your journey to freedom.

Learning to love ourselves appropriately is vital in winning the fight against insecurity. It is not the kind of self-love that keeps us focused on the person in the mirror. It is not a narcissistic obsession that keeps us taking selfies because we are just that into ourselves. It is the love for ourselves that frees us to live in the light, to live in the freedom Christ died to give us. "Whoever does not love does not know God, because God is love. This is how God showed his love among us: He sent his one and only Son into the world that we might live through him. This is love: not that we loved God, but that he loved us and sent his Son as an atoning sacrifice for our sins. Dear friends, since God so loved us, we also ought to love one another." 1 John 4:8-11.

And this includes ourselves. God has always loved us, and still does. There is nothing you can do to get God to love you more and there is nothing you can do to get God to love you less. He accepts you under the grace of Jesus Christ. When I am loved, I have the capacity to love others. Not from my own strength, but from the strength His love gives me. If you want to learn how to love yourself, start in the presence of love. "God is love. Whoever lives in love lives in God, and God in him. ... There is no fear in love. But perfect love drives out fear, ... *We love because he first loved us.*" 1 John 4:8-19 (emphasis mine)

Trust and love work together in our journey to overcome our insecurities. You can trust God's Word as truth because you have spent enough time with Him to realize He is trustworthy. In that time you spend, you find Love — God Himself — and love leads us to freedom. But it starts with an active choice to trust what God's Word says about us is true, and it is an active choice to love ourselves despite how we feel. The battle for freedom may be fought in the head, but it is won in the heart.

My prayer for you, dear friend, is that you will realize the prize of freedom is love and the prize of love is freedom. When you can rest in the knowledge that you are loved by Love Himself, you will be free, and when you are free, you will be able to love yourself and others more fully than you ever thought possible. When you spend time in the presence of love it will rub off on you. You will discover a power rising up from within you like a spiritual adrenaline giving you the strength to do what you never thought you could do on your own. This love will propel you, to overcome whatever obstacles lie in your path to becoming the person you now see is possible for you to become. Old fears will fall away like loosened chains because there is no fear in love. Apprehension will be swallowed up with faith because in His presence yours will be strengthened. His love will free you and fuel your forward action. Nothing will be able to hold you back when you stay connected to this Love. You will be motivated to lay down your insecurities and be free. There won't be room for fear and lies because you will fill your heart with truth. You will be able to become all that God has created you to be and live free.

Free indeed.

Take a deeper step: In_Security

1. How would you describe your relationship with God? Is He more of a stranger, acquaintance or close friend? Explain your answer.

2. Why do you think people struggle with loving themselves? Have you struggled with learning to love yourself? Why?

3. How do trust and love work together to help free us from our insecurities and bondage?

4. What will be your next step in continuing the journey of freedom you have begun?

Acknowledgments

It seems impossible to acknowledge all the people who helped me through the process of writing this book. I could say thank you to everyone I have ever come into contact with, because I believe I can learn from anyone if I have the right perspective. And learn, I have. So to those who have helped indirectly and those whose influence helped shaped this book directly, I thank you.

To:

Cody — My dreamer. You never doubted me, but your ideas and contagious vision for our family inspire me every day. You make me want to be better. Thank you for bathing kids and putting them to bed on nights I was writing, for bringing me coffee and tea and snacks, and keeping the laundry going, just so I could stay in the chair and work. Thank you for being my keeper. I'm lucky to call you mine.

My children — My prayer is that you will learn to love Jesus Christ with your whole heart, serve Him with your life, and let nothing hold you back from reaching your full potential.

My parents — for raising me to love Jesus Christ, sacrificing so I would have as many opportunities as I could, and always supporting me in the pursuit of my passions.

Siblings & In-laws— for loving me unconditionally, accepting me for who I am, and always encouraging me to be better.

Scott Williams—You believed in me, saw my potential, and never stopped showing me how to dream big and think bigger.

My friends — Brandie Reisman, Abi Martin, Troy and Megann Frazier, Wendi O'Connor, Jeremy and Kelsey Baldwin, Jamie and Lauren Wheat, Jonathan and Lisa Stapp, Jodi Grawunder, MaryMartha Ford, Jana Brown and Sherri Reeves, for praying for me during months of writing and encouraging me to keep going.

Nancy Henderson — For your hours of editing and making me sound better than I would have on my own.

Friends, volunteers, and staff from the Northwest Campus of Life.Church and those who shared your struggles and stories with me (too many to list) — without your relationship I wouldn't be the same person I am today.

Jesus —You pushed me to write this book even when I didn't want to. Your loving grace continually compelled me to obey your calling even when I doubted my ability. This is my worship to You, and my obedience.

Appendix A

Resources for a Deeper Study on Self-awareness

Leadership and Self-deception: Getting Out of the Box by The Arbinger Institute

What Got you Here Won't Get you There: How Successful People Become Even More Successful by Marshall Goldsmith and Mark Reiter

The EQ Edge: Emotional Intelligence and Your Success by Steven J. Stein, PH.D. and Howard E. Book, M.D.

Emotional Intelligence 2.0 by Travis Bradberry and Jean Greaves

Now, Discover Your Strengths by Marcus Buckingham and Donald O. Clifton, Ph.D.

Strengths Finder 2.0 by Tom Rath

Online Resources:

Keirsey Personality testing

Myer-Briggs Personality testing

DISC Personality testing

Spiritual Gift testing

Appendix B

Don't self-sabotage your freedom

The decision to make a change can be a frightening thing, and the enemy will come at us even stronger than before. Remember, a free person is a dangerous person to the enemy, so he will try to destroy our progress through self-sabotage.

I am a recovering self-saboteur. As I have overcome this bad habit, I have noticed a few reasons we may find it easy to fall prey to sabotaging our own best intentions.

We believe we're not worth it, or we don't deserve it. This is a common lie of the enemy, especially among women. Relational sabotage is wrapped up in this lie: "Go ahead, settle for what is less than best. You're not worth the wait... the trouble... the work. You do not deserve to feel loved... pretty... fought for... pursued." Fill in the blank. If we fall for this lie, we will self-sabotage by selling ourselves short. If no one has ever told you, I'm telling you now: You are worth the fight and the time it takes to make a change.

We allow our feelings or emotions to dictate our actions. Most women, and maybe a few men, know this all too well. Many of our goals, dreams and visions are delayed, destroyed or dismissed when we allow our emotions to control us. Don't get me wrong, feelings and emotions can be good things. God made us emotional, but our emotions and feelings can sabotage us if we do not bring them under His authority, focusing them in a positive way. A Bible reading plan I followed recently talked about our emotions and how they travel 80,000 times faster than our thoughts travel. Knowing this can help us understand why we sometimes act on our feelings even when we know the right things to do. Ever wonder why the Bible says to "Guard your heart."? (Proverbs 4:23) Because from it springs our feelings and emotions. It is not only talking about guarding it from outside predators, but also guarding the emotions that may want to come out of it, if they are not in line with God's leadership. A mentor of mine likes to say, "feelings are rarely our friends." When we allow our feelings to control us we never know what may happen or where we may end up. Finding freedom from insecurity is not a practice in feelings, but a practice in choice.

Laziness. Of course, it is easier to skip our Bible reading, not practice our sport, craft or art, or sit down and accomplish what God has called us to do. It takes a lot less effort to let our thoughts run wild, or our mouths say what they want. Doing what we know we need to do is the harder thing. If it wasn't hard, it wouldn't be worth it. We have to get off the couch of our mind and stand up for our freedom. No one else is going to do it for us! We must not allow laziness to cripple something

God is calling us to do. "What one does is what counts. Not what one had the intention of doing."—Picasso.

Fear of change. Oftentimes, it is this fear that keeps us taking one step forward and two steps back. We impede our progress because we fear how progress might change our lives. We fear failure, but we also fear success. We keep ourselves in our comfort zones, even though we are screaming to get out. We are playing tug-of-war with our flesh and spirit and the one who is going to win is the one we feed more. If our flesh is stronger, we will never change. We will stay in the prison of insecurity because that is where it is safe. It is what we have always known. As He asked the man waiting to be healed, Jesus is asking us, "Do you want to be free?" We keep ourselves living an okay life, when God has an unimaginably magnificent life waiting for us on the other side of change. Yes, change is scary. It is the unknown that stretches itself out across the expanse of our mind and keeps us from taking that first step forward. It is okay to feel afraid, but step out anyway. It is only when we step out of our comfort zone— step out of our bondage— that we will discover the life God designed for us all along.

References

Donald Miller, *Blue Like Jazz*, Nashville, Thomas Nelson Publishers, A Division of Thomas Nelson, Inc. (2003) page 231

Bradberry T. & Greaves J. *Emotional Intelligence 2.0*, San Diego TalentSmart (2009) Page 16,17

John Eldridge, *Wild at Heart*, Nashville, Thomas Nelson, a registered trademark of Thomas Nelson, Inc. (2001) Page 62

53771057R00106

Made in the USA
Lexington, KY
18 July 2016